As we anticipate the dawn of a new century and the inevitable changes and discoveries to come, we should reflect on life at the beginning of the twentieth century.

Yesteryear's Child tells of everyday life from town to farm: the routines of cleaning and cooking, the realities of disease and its cures, celebrations and disappointments, the details of entertainments, clothing, and childhood. This easy-to-read account of life before the First World War evokes the paradox of times past which seem so like our own while at the same time seeming so different.

Much like Robert Shellenberger's **WAGONS WEST: Trail Tales 1848, YESTERYEAR'S CHILD: Golden Days & Summer Nights** is a continuum of HERITAGE WEST BOOKS' social history series dedicated to capturing a gentle understanding and appreciation of our forefathers' world.

Yesteryear's Child

Golden Days & Summer Nights

by
Phoebe Louise Westwood
with
Richard W. Rohrbacher, Ph.D.

HERITAGE WEST BOOKS
Stockton, California

ISBN 0-9623048-7-5

Library of Congress Catalog Number 93-077688

Cover Design by AR Design
        Stockton, California
Manuscript typing by Lydia Kim
Copyediting by Lois Owen
Production Editing and Design
        by Suzanne Goldberg

Published by   HERITAGE WEST BOOKS
                306 Regent Court
                Stockton, CA 95204

Cover photograph: Phoebe Louise Westwood (1896-1984),
        circa 1908 *(Rohrbacher Family Collection)*

In memory of Phoebe's tenth grandchild,
Nancy Clair Rohrbacher
1955-1967

Contents

Preface

The manuscript you are about to read is a labor of love on the part of a number of people. In its first draft it was a handwritten document started about 1979 and completed about 1980 while Mom was living in Fresno, California. At that time she asked me to look it over and see what I could do about editing it and getting it into shape to send out to her children and grandchildren. This is a first person account of what life was like while she was growing up in a small, northern California town at the turn of the twentieth century.

Her granddaughter Kathy Graham-Crouthamel most graciously offered to type the first draft from Mom's cursive version. During my convalescence from a serious illness in 1981 I was able to edit the first draft and make suggestions for changes and additions. Over the next three years, as her strength allowed, this intelligent and loving woman worked on the second draft which we found, nearly finished, in her desk at the time of her death in 1984.

In preparation for a family reunion in Washington State in 1986, I was motivated to get out Mom's manuscript, dust it off, and start the demanding job of attempting to piece her suggested revisions together into a logical order. In the process I found two cassettes containing 180 minutes of interviews with my mother. I had recorded her remarks over her breakfast table one morning in the late 1970s. I was able to work much of the information contained in that interview into this manuscript.

Additional material for this account was gleaned from letters and an unpublished family history compiled by my mother's late brother, Dr. Willard S. Westwood (1893-1974). Much of the information in this book pertaining to genealogy was either supported by his writings or was confirmed from his research. His information went a long way toward helping to flesh out this account.

Mom, or Grandma Phoebe, as most of our family knew her, lived a long and interesting life. My hope is that you, the reader, will enjoy and learn something from this account of her formative years. This is her statement about a moment in history through which she lived. It wasn't necessarily a "gentler, kinder age" than the one we know, but her growing up time was entirely unlike what we are experiencing during this last decade of the 1900s. This is a chronicle which includes the impressions of a loving and fascinating woman. In a sense, it's a book of remembrances.

My only regret is that Mom didn't live long enough to see the finished product. I am sure she would have been very proud to see her thoughts and reminiscences in print. I like to think she would have been pleased with my labors and its eventual outcome. If she had read this version before it went to the printer, I am sure it would have triggered more memories which she would have insisted be added to her story. They would have made this account even richer than it is.

I especially want to acknowledge Lillian Pinker of the Butte County Historical Society who assisted me by finding many of the photographs used to illustrate this volume. I also want to thank her for the encouragement she offered during the writing of the final draft of this book.

Finally, I want to express gratitude to Frances, my wife, for her help in editing my editing. I even thank her for nagging me to take the time necessary to piece this manuscript together.

In addition, I offer special thanks to my daughter, Roseanne Rohrbacher-Grey, who willingly took on the onerous task of doing much of the early proofreading and locating many typos in the final drafts.

Finally, sincere and special appreciation to my editor/publisher, Sylvia Sun Minnick, who recognized the value of this manuscript and offered to publish it. She gave unstintingly of her time and encouragement.

RICHARD W. ROHRBACHER, PH.D.

1

Our Town

I was born at home on April 12, 1896, in Oroville, a small town in Butte County, California. My home town came into existence shortly after 1848 when gold was discovered on the South Fork of the American River near Coloma. This momentous event took place in January of 1848. James W. Marshall, while supervising the digging of the mill tailrace for a new sawmill being built for John Sutter, saw a glint of yellow metal in the water and picked it up. To his surprise it turned out to be a gold nugget. That was the beginning of the mad rush into the Republic of California.

During the next few years, thousands of people from all over the world streamed into that part of the Sierra foothills which eventually made up the Northern and Southern mines. They were in a headlong quest which came to be known as California's 1849 Gold Rush.

Ophir, meaning Gold Town, is the name by which Oroville was originally known. The name was changed shortly after California became a state. Our town was a fairly typical small California town at the end of the nineteenth century. It is located in Butte County on the North Fork of the Feather River near the top of the Sacramento Valley and is ringed to the north by a series of table mountains in the foothills of the northern Sierra Nevada Mountains. It had three distinct sections: the flat part, along Broderick Street with the river at its back, Depot Hill, and Flour Mill Hill. The town was mostly residential except for the few blocks devoted to business.

Oroville was and still is the county seat of Butte County. The main street was Montgomery Street's three-block span. It had two dry goods stores, one combined ice cream parlor and candy store, two grocery stores, one green grocer, one bakery, one shoe store, a livery stable, a couple of doctors, a dentist, one pharmacy or apothecary shop as we called it, a millinery shop, a hotel with an annex for gold miners, one Chinese restaurant, one Chinese and one steam laundry, one bank, seven saloons, and an undertaker. The courthouse sat in the center of a square block between Huntoon and Lincoln Streets, bordered by Montgomery Street on the north and Bird Street on the south. The courthouse was surrounded by shade trees and elevated green lawns.

Oroville was a town where people took great pride in their yards and gardens. Nearly every house had a decorative fence enclosing its yard. They were either white pickets or wrought iron. Because of the extremely hot summers, most residents planted shade trees, especially on the south and west sides of their homes. These were stuck in the ground in every available place. Even though the town was dusty and hotter than blazes in the summer and wet, muddy, and cold as Billy be damned in the winter, it was a place one could be proud of.

In the summertime the unpaved streets were blanketed with thick red dust. In winter the dust became a quagmire of sticky red mud. The streets were lined on both sides with raised wooden sidewalks. They were about two feet above the street to facilitate the loading and unloading of wagons.

Raised sidewalks served at least two other purposes. One was to keep pedestrians out of the mud or the dust of the streets and the second was to serve as a convenience for those who had too much to drink. Imbibers could sit with their feet resting in the gutter until they had sobered sufficiently to stagger home or had become steady enough on their feet to find their way into the next saloon. I assume this is where the saying, "He ended up in the gutter" or, "He has both feet in the gutter" came from. My grandfather Westwood had a saying when referring to someone who had fallen pretty low through drink. "He'll be down in the gutter pretty soon, pickin' with the chickens." One additional but unintended use of the raised sidewalks was for the convenience of children. They made a great place to sit during a town parade or celebration.

At the turn of the century there were about 3,000 people living in and near the township. Of these, about one-third were Chinese, mostly men, who had been brought in to help build the railroad through the Feather River Canyon and who had remained after the project was finished. There were four Jewish families who owned businesses; two families of Italians, one was a greengrocer, while the other grew row crops and ran a restaurant; one Negro family, the man was the janitor at the bank; and finally a household of Germans who ran Oroville's only real bakery. The remainder of our town was made up of Scots, English, Irish, or Welsh.

Saturday night was the highlight of everyone's week. All the stores stayed open until nine, and everyone, and I mean everyone, promenaded downtown after supper. The women did their week's shopping on that evening and visited with friends they met on the street. Just before nine o'clock, as part of the Saturday night ritual, the women and children, whose husbands and fathers worked in the shops, stopped at the ice cream parlor for sodas or a banana split.

The children ganged together in one corner of the ice cream parlor to chat, and mothers huddled together in another corner to catch up on the latest town gossip. After closing their shops, the menfolk joined their families.

For youngsters, the Saturday night excursion was an exciting experience. Things became positively sensational when Mother clutched our hands extra tight and attempted to pull us as rapidly as possible past the half doors of the saloons. Her aim was to get us by the swinging doors as fast as our legs would carry us. I usually managed to hold back long enough to get a quick peek under the doors in order to see what was happening inside.

The saloon, with its polished brass rails and spittoons, was an extraordinary and thrilling world to my young eyes and ears. It was full of bright lights made hazy by tobacco smoke, glistening mirrors, a hodgepodge of smells, and a potpourri of attractive sounds. If I was quick enough, I could catch a hasty glimpse of one of the life sized paintings of reclining and completely naked ladies that invariably hung behind the long mahogany bars. These saloons seemed almost theatrical in spirit with their lively piano music, clinking of glasses, cigar smoke, and exotic smells, combined with the sounds of deep masculine laughter.

Mother would admonish us to ignore any off-color remarks from inebriated and befuddled miners we might encounter. We were severely forewarned to be especially careful to avoid colliding with them as they staggered down the sidewalks.

For the most part, the miners were a sad but harmless lot. They lived solitary and very lonely lives. They came down from the mountains on Saturday nights to blow off steam. The first thing they did was take a bath and get a shave. After they had changed into clean clothes and were all spruced up and doused by the barber with copious amounts of bay rum tonic, they began their quest for an exciting evening on the town.

The town drinking establishments offered bright lights, a free lunch, piano music or even a small band, singing, dancing, and plenty to drink. The biggest attraction from the men's point of view was female companionship for a nominal price.

Inasmuch as the saloons were, by law, closed all day Sunday, the miners had a compelling urgency to make hay while they could and cram a week's celebrating into one night. They knew, no matter how drunk they got, they could sleep it off the next day.

Typical group of miners heading for the "digging" in the hills east of Oroville, circa 1890. *(Courtesy Butte County Historical Society)*

Many of the miners knew my mother as she was born and raised in the nearby community of Magalia in the mining country. When the men recognized her, no matter how much they were into their cups, they swept off their hats, bowed deeply, and then approached us. They shook hands while saying something like, "Maggie Smeaton, here you are, all growed up! And a handsome woman you are too! Look at you now, with two youngens of your own!"

Often they dug into their pockets and pulled out two silver dollars. They gave my brother and me each a big round silver cartwheel. To our displeasure and great disappointment our penurious Mother never allowed us to spend it. A silver dollar was big money in those days, especially for a youngster. She said, "I'll just put this away for you for something special." When we complained, she retorted, "You'll be glad I saved this for you when the time comes that you really need it. You just wait and see!" To prove her point she reached into her handbag, pulled out her multi-pocketed change purse, and snapped it open. The silver dollars were slipped into one compartment and two five-cent pieces were taken out of another. She carefully placed a nickel in the palm of each of our hands. This was ours to spend that evening. Five cents bought an enormous bag of walking around candy.

As much as I disagreed at the time, my practical mother was right as usual. The dollars came in handy later on for buying birthday and Christmas presents.

Mother told us that when she was a child most of the miners left the mountains when the first snow flew and headed for a warmer place like Sacramento. Many of them even took a river boat down the Sacramento River to Stockton. Some went as far away as San Francisco.

Every miner had a donkey he used as a pack animal. Before a man left the mountains for the winter, he found a local child who agreed to feed and care for his pack animal during the long winter months. The children were delighted to be able to earn a little extra money. As a bonus for their effort the children had their own donkey to ride to school all winter long and to serve as a playmate until the spring thaw. It was an unhappy day indeed when the owner drifted back into town to reclaim his animal.

Oroville had two schools. One was the Bird Street Grammar School located on the corner of First Avenue between Bird and Pine. The other was Oroville Union High School on the corner of Second Avenue and Robinson Street. We were understandably proud of our high school because it was accredited to The Leland Stanford, Jr. University and the University of California.

Grammar school was a nine-year stint. Those who persevered and finished were awarded a diploma and became a part of the town's educated elite. When a young graduate received his or her grammar school diploma it was an occasion for a family celebration. To have a child graduate from grammar school was an accomplishment for which the entire family had every right to be self-satisfied, and the certificate was framed and proudly hung on the parlor wall. Of the young people who managed to finish grammar school, only a handful went on to high school.

Secondary school was reserved for those families who aspired to have their children become teachers, doctors, engineers, or lawyers. For anyone else, higher education was considered a waste of time.

On the East Coast I understand things were different, but in California we had our own way of doing things. After all, a ninth grade graduate had read a great deal of literature, had learned algebra, poetry, some Latin, a touch of chemistry and physics, and was now more than prepared for the world of work or, in the case of girls, for marriage and motherhood.

Unfortunately, the Chinese children were not allowed, by California state law, to attend public school.

The Caucasian children who attended grammar school rarely went beyond the sixth grade. However, my family truly believed in the benefits of higher education. My mother and father, who were both quite proud to have been through grammar school, saw to it that my brother finished high school. At great financial sacrifice they sent the two of us on to the University of California at Berkeley.

The Bird Street School, circa 1900. *(Courtesy Butte County Historical Society)*

We boasted four churches in Oroville. They were Episcopal, Methodist, Congregational and Roman Catholic.

My family were Episcopalians and attended St. John's Church on Second Avenue. A communicant in the Episcopal Church, by Congregational and Methodist standards, was considered nearly as bad as a Roman Catholic. They took great exception to the fact that we, along with the Catholics, danced, played cards, and did not wear a white ribbon on our lapel to signify we had signed our yearly pledge of abstinence from liquor. According to my friends, whose families didn't happen to be either Catholic or Episcopalians, our chances of ever getting into Heaven were pretty slim, unless we were lucky enough to die during Lent.

Regardless of religious differences, our neighbors were our close friends. We shared recipes; passed jam, jellies, cakes, cookies, pies and casseroles over the fence; exchanged plants and cuttings; and helped out in case of need or sickness.

There wasn't much poverty in those days. It seemed that anyone who wanted to work had a job of some kind. Even the young, if they were industrious, had ways of making pocket money. To earn a nickel, one could run errands, cut lawns, clean out storm gutters, or sweep up the walks in front of the homes of the elderly. Sometimes, even if you didn't get a nickel, you did the neighborly chore anyway.

Chinatown was a separate town entirely and was set apart, so to speak, from where the "Americans" lived. As children, we were never allowed to set foot in Chinatown except once a year; that was in February, during Chinese New Year. Even then we were allowed on Broderick Street only while accompanied by our parents. The centerpiece of that part of Oroville was the Chinese Temple. It was completed in the early 1860s, when there were an estimated 10,000 Chinese living in and around Oroville.

Originally the majority of the Chinese lived about eight miles northeast of town, up the Feather River at a place called Bidwell Bar. After a disastrous fire in the 1850s destroyed most of the Chinese settlement, they moved downstream to Oroville. Their temple, well preserved, is located on Broderick Street next to the levee.

When a major flood in 1907 swirled through Oroville, the Chinese community bore the brunt of the destruction. After this disaster most of the Chinese left Oroville.

The Chinese Temple located near the Feather River Levee on Broderick Street, circa 1900. *(Courtesy Butte County Historical Society)*

Chinese New Year was a gala week of celebration which everyone eagerly awaited. Everyone in town went to watch the parade and to enjoy the bombastic theatre with its unfamiliar and exotic music. The propmen were different from anything we know in Western theatre. They dressed in black costumes and popped onto the stage holding a prop whenever they were needed. I learned later in life that propmen on stage is traditional in Chinese theatre and they are ignored by the Chinese audience.

Chinese New Year was an opportunity for sightseeing in a culture very different from our western traditions. It also gave us an opportunity to admire the Chinese children in their gaily embroidered clothing.

For a few pennies we were able to purchase all kinds of delectable edibles. We sucked sugarcane, chewed on Chinese candy, munched candied watermelon rind and coconut, and ate lichee nuts and almond paste cookies.

For a few additional pennies we bought a grocery bag full of strings of firecrackers and a supply of punks with which to light them. We didn't understand everything that was going on, but we joined in the spirit of the festival by banging off our noise makers along with everyone else.

My brother used to scare my mother by lighting his firecrackers while holding them between his thumb and index finger and then throwing them at the last second before they went off. We held back a supply of fire-crackers to be used to celebrate the Fourth of July.

Much to my parents' mortification, the shortest route from our home to Chinatown took us through the "red light district," which consisted of only one sporting house. This was a beautiful Victorian home trimmed with ornate and meticulously designed and executed gingerbread dec-orations, complete with a widow's walk around the top.

This establishment was run by a Madam Lola. When we passed Lola's place while with our parents, we averted our eyes and didn't ask questions. Of course we didn't ask questions because we knew we wouldn't get answers on such a taboo subject.

2

My Family

I had only one brother and no sisters. My brother, born in 1893, was three years older than I. His name was Willard Smeaton, his middle name being my mother's maiden name. We usually called him Bill.

The four of us lived in a small, five-room house next to the grammar school on Robinson Street. Grandfather David Westwood gave the house to my parents as a wedding gift, and it served us very well until, when I was about five, my mother inherited $4,000 from the Smeaton side of the family. With that money my parents built our new home.

We called our new home "The Big House," which it was, compared to our smaller five-room home. Our new abode had four bedrooms and all of the modern conveniences of that time, including electric lights and a flush toilet which was located on the back porch. At the turn of the century, no one would consider having a commode in the main part of the house.

The bathroom, which was separate from the toilet, was next to the kitchen. It was a small room, only large enough for the tub and a towel rack. We had only cold water piped into the bathroom so water was heated in five-gallon buckets on the kitchen stove, toted into the bathroom and added to the cold water. Placing the bathroom next to the kitchen made it a little easier to fill the bathtub.

My mother was a very nervous person and was deathly afraid of fire. Our living room table was covered with a floor length chenille cover with fringe on it. Prior to our having electricity, there was an oil lamp sitting in the middle. My mother was terrified I might pull the table over and the lamp would smash and burn the house down, killing me and the entire family. To relieve my mother's fear, my father had installed electric lights which were the ugliest things imaginable. They hung from the ceiling on a strand of braided wire with a single bulb dangling at the end. To dress them up a little, Mother made her own shades cut out of colored construction paper glued together down the sides. For trim, she used elegant paper cut into elaborate designs. When she was through, the lamps didn't look half bad.

We had one electric light hanging from the middle of the ceilings in the dining room, in each of the bedrooms, and in the kitchen, plus the one I've already mentioned in the living room.

In 1908 our first telephone was installed, a big wooden instrument with a crank on the side. It hung on the wall of the kitchen, which was the hub of family activity, so there were no secret or private conversations carried on by telephone.

Uncle John used to come in quite often from his farm to visit. He usually had a number of telephone calls he needed to make to business people in Oroville. After he had loudly informed the central operator what number he wanted and had been connected to his party, he stood back a good three feet from the instrument and, while holding the receiver away from his ear, shouted at the top of his lungs at the mouthpiece. I had the distinct feeling he was scared to death of the dang thing. My brother and I had a hard time to keep from laughing and left the room in fear he might catch us having fun at his expense.

I can still see my mother scolding him. She stood, hands on hips and said, "John, you don't need the telephone. Open the window and shout. They'll be sure to hear you."

The number of people in our household grew steadily. First it went to five when my mother's mother was widowed for the third time and came to live with us. Then my cousin Ernest joined us when he left the farm to work for my father. A short time later when Aunt Lottie's husband died, she and her son Lloyd came for a visit which lasted for many months. Bill and I didn't mind at all because Lloyd was our age and it was great having him as part of our crowd.

Over the next few years a string of cousins from the farm came to live with us. They arrived one or two at a time to attend high school. Living became a bit crowded at times, but with extra beds set up in our oversized bedrooms, things worked out just fine.

We all did our share of the chores around the house. If you didn't, you were soon told about it. We were expected to pull our own weight in order to keep the house running smoothly. As tough as it was at the time, this hard work and cooperation resulted in a clean and efficiently operating household.

My farmer uncles paid for their sons' and daughters' board and room with farm produce—fresh fruit, meat and chickens, vegetables, butter, milk, eggs, cured hams and bacon, and anything else that happened to be in season. When the uncles came to town, they had their noon meal with us. To my great happiness, they often brought my namesake, Grandmother Phoebe with them. She spent the day with us while the men carried on their business in town.

My father was one of six sons and my mother had three sisters and one brother which meant I had loads of aunts and uncles and a total of eighteen cousins. I was the youngest and came in for my share of being both petted and teased.

My grandmothers fulfilled two entirely different functions in my young life. Margaret, my mother's mother, was addressed by the rather formal title of Grandmother. My father's mother was referred to as Grandma.

Grandmother lived a rather tragic life by any day's standards. She grew up in the family hotel until she was fifteen at which point she married a hard-rock miner named Edward Smeaton. She had my mother at the age of sixteen and my Aunt Frankie a year later. She was widowed when my mother was four. After that, Grandmother married a man named Davis and had a daughter, my Aunt Lottie. Mr. Davis died of "Miner's Consumption," leaving Grandmother a widow for a second time. By then she had three children. Grandmother married a third miner named Robert McDonald and had two more children, Lillian and Rob.

The saying goes, "Bad luck always comes in threes." Grandmother's life surely illustrated this. Mr. McDonald sickened and died of the same miners' disease as her first two husbands. Grandmother McDonald was a widow three times over before she was forty years old.

Grandfather Edward Smeaton (1832-1874), circa 1870. *(Rohrbacher Family Collection)*

She took on many of the responsibilities that had previously been performed by my mother. She bathed me, made all of my clothes, brushed my hair and braided it into tight shiny braids. She put me to bed, then listened to my prayers. Grandmother helped me with my lessons and made sure my homework for the next day's classes was complete and done neatly. She also paid great attention to my table manners, etiquette, and deportment. To all intents and purposes Grandmother McDonald was a second mother. I respected and minded her the same as I did my own mother.

Grandma Westwood was a midwife and a practical nurse, and she delivered both my brother and me. She had a large frame and, as my brother described her, was "well upholstered." We never managed to sit on her lap because there wasn't any room. She was kind, had a sunny disposition, loved people and liked to have them about. She didn't have a mean bone in her body.

After Grandfather Westwood died in 1903, whenever I went to the farm for a visit with Grandma, I slept in her huge feather bed, cuddled up against her ample frame. She often took me visiting to other farms, and on the way, she permitted me to hold the reins and drive her light-weight buggy called a phaeton. She also allowed me to go bareback riding on a gentle old horse named Nell.

When Grandma baked bread, she cut the heel off of a loaf of freshly baked bread, slathered it with newly churned butter, sprinkled it with sugar and cinnamon, and permitted me to eat it—even between meals. I can still smell the yeast and taste the essence of her wonderful home baked bread.

In the afternoons we had tea and toast. She brewed a special brand of strong English tea and served it "white" with milk and sugar. She even allowed me to dunk my toast. Dunking was an extra special treat because I was never allowed to do it at home.

My most cherished memories of Grandma were her stories. She told the most delightful tales one could ever imagine. They were more beautiful than any I have ever read in books. In her rich Midland English accent she told me what life was like in her home town of Worcester. Her favorite stories were about the ghosts that haunted the castles.

Many years later when I made my first trip to England, I was emotionally shaken because I had such a strong feeling I had been there before. The hedgerows, the half-timbered farm houses, and the chimney pots that I saw from the boat train on its way into London all looked familiar. I finally figured out that Grandma's stories and her vivid descriptions of the beauties of her English countryside had sunk deeply into my subconsciousness.

I sat at Grandma's knee on a padded foot stool while she regaled me with her stories. Many times during the telling, she slipped her hand into a deep pocket in her petticoat and pulled out a piece of candy. This wonderful pocket held an endless supply of little bags of hore-hound, peppermint, or lemon drops. She held up one of the candies and said, "Shut thy peepers, Phoebe girl! Now, open thy gob and stick out thy lolliker." Then one of her delicious candies dropped onto my tongue. Her stories were as appetizing to my ears as were her delectable sweets to my tongue. I adored Grandma and every moment spent with her was sheer happiness.

Grandfather Westwood was an entirely different matter. I loved him, but I was somewhat fearful of him. He was a blacksmith and very, very English. He was a small man and slight of build. Despite his lack of size, he was strong, wiry and quick of action. He was completely bald with a fringe of white hair over his ears which blended into a large square-cut beard without a moustache. In his old age, and that is the only way I knew him, he was deaf as a post. This may have been due to the years of being subjected to the ringing of his blacksmith hammer as it struck the anvil. He was an extremely industrious and hard working man.

He was born in Bromsgrove, England, which is about five miles from Worcester, the town from which

Grandma Phoebe came. I never learned if they or their families knew each other before leaving England.

Grandma Phoebe Ellen Westwood, neé Bromley (1836-1911), circa 1900. *(Rohrbacher Family Collection)*

At four o'clock on the dot, he came into the house for tea. The first thing he did was take off his work jumper, wash his hands and face, then put on a white stock. (This is an old-fashioned stiff shirt front with collar. Some men used them in place of a collar and tie.) Next he slipped into a black alpaca jacket. Both items hung, at the ready, on a hook in the kitchen. Then he pulled off his boots and changed into carpet slippers.

When he appeared in the parlor, Grandma was ready to serve an elegant English tea. This consisted of a pot of tea with a cozy to keep it warm, Devonshire cream, thin cut tomato or cucumber sandwiches with the crust trimmed off, scones, buttered bread, and all kinds of exquisite little cakes and cookies. (Grandma never called them cookies. To her they were "biscuits.") This spread of luscious edibles was served on a hand-embroidered linen cloth.

Immediately after he finished his tea, Grandfather lay down for exactly fifteen minutes by the clock, no more, no less. When the allotted time had passed, he changed back into his work clothes and returned to whatever task he had been tending to before tea.

As much as I loved the elegant goodies served at tea time, this was, for me, a trying time because of my fear of Grandfather. If I became too talkative, he looked me straight in the eyes and said, "Children are to be seen and not heard!" I can still see him locking eyes with me, as if to dare me to do something inappropriate. With that kind of a warning I minded my manners while he was in the room. On rare occasions he softened and smiled at me, patted me gently on the head, and called me "Little Princess." Despite the fact that he was a small man, I can still feel the size and strength of his large blacksmith's hands on my head. I now attribute his gruffness towards me as being due, at least in part, to the fact that he had six sons and no daughters. He probably wasn't sure how he should act around a little girl.

Despite my grandfather's age, he put in long working days. The men worked until after sundown. When it became too dark to see, he, Uncle John and the other men came into the house to clean up for supper.

Grandfather was a Forty-Niner in every sense of the word. He came to California in 1849 and stayed about two years. He spent most of that time in El Dorado County. To my knowledge he never worked in a mine. He found he could make much more money letting the miners do the digging and pay him to ply his trade of blacksmithing. He liked to work for the miners, especially when the pay was in gold dust.

Sometime between 1851 and 1852 he left California and went east, probably to New Orleans to meet his family. Eventually he came up the Mississippi with them to a place close to St. Louis, Missouri. Sometime during their early lives, while still living in England, the Westwoods and the Bromleys had converted to the Mormon religion.

In 1852 Grandfather Westwood married Grandma Phoebe, whose maiden name was Bromley. The wedding took place in Missouri. Shortly after their marriage they made the trek to Utah in an organized company of "Saints." On many different occasions I heard my grandfather tell about coming out to the Utah Territory with the Mormons. He told of skirmishes along the way with Indians who constantly tried to steal or scatter their animals. He talked about the men and how they had constant guard duty at night for fear of surprise Indian attacks.

Evidently, for a number of years, things went along quite well for the young family. They had three sons, John in 1853, Joseph in 1855, and David in 1857.

In the fall of 1857 a terrible thing happened in southwest Utah at Mountain Meadows. There, more than one hundred men, women, and children in a wagon train heading for California were murdered. This incident is known by historians as the Mountain Meadows Massacre.

According to Grandfather the mass murder was organized by a group of Mormons who were helped by some Indians. Everyone in the wagon train was killed except for the very small children.

All Latter Day Saints men from that part of Utah Territory were in the Mormon militia. The unit to which my grandfather belonged was ordered to Mountain Meadows to help bury the dead. To my grandfather's shock some of the people he helped bury were Mormons who were well known to him.

Grandfather David Westwood, aka
Darius West (1826-1903), circa 1895.
(Rohrbacher Family Collection)

This horrible experience gave him the motivation to leave the Mormons and return to the Anglicans. He eventually packed up his wife and family of, by this time, four sons, and returned to California in 1864.

From then on Grandfather disliked the Mormons and everything they stood for. Whenever a Mormon relative came to Oroville for a visit, Grandfather, in order to show his contempt for them, turned his rocking chair to the wall. In this way he could enjoy rocking at the end of the work day, but wouldn't have to look at them. Because he was deaf, he didn't have to listen to them either. He wouldn't turn his chair back around until the visitor left.

When my Westwood grandparents arrived in Oroville they camped near Bed Rock. This is now opposite Oroville's Fifth Avenue on the bank of the Feather River. Their campsite was at a crossing of the river for teams. This afforded Grandfather an excellent opportunity to ply his trade as a blacksmith.

Grandfather had a bit of the rover in him. When the War Between the States broke out, he enlisted in Company B of the Sixth Regiment of the California Volunteers. For some reason known only to himself he enlisted under the name of Darius West and served as a private for eighteen months. I now hold the theory that he changed his name because the California Volunteers were headed for the Utah Territory to keep the telegraph and supply lines open between California and the East. The Union badly needed California's gold and copper and silver from Nevada in order to win the war. With a price put on his head by the Mormons, he could hardly return to Utah under his real name.

When Grandfather went off to war, Grandma Phoebe packed up their four sons and went along with him. She earned her keep by cooking, doing soldiers' laundry, and acting as a nurse. How in the world she accomplished this with four children, the oldest being only about eleven, is beyond me. Women of her generation were surely made of rigorous stuff.

After the War of the Rebellion, my Westwood grandparents moved out to Central House, halfway between Oroville and Marysville, where they homesteaded the section of land which Grandfather received for his Civil War service. This piece of land later proved to be among the richest of all agricultural lands in California.

In many ways Grandfather was a character who also possessed a will of iron. He never rode on a wagon after it was loaded despite the fact his farm was twelve miles from Oroville. When he took a wagon either in or out of town with a load, he invariably walked at the head of the horses. When asked why he never rode, he answered,

"The beasties have enough to haul this load without carrying a man with two good legs."

Grandfather was also a Bible student. He claimed he studied the Bible so he could argue with the visiting Episcopal priest when he came out to Central House to conduct once-a-month communion services. Grandfather invited him for Sunday dinner after those monthly services so he could argue some fine points of the Bible with him.

Mother's family were also Forty-Niners. Peter Woolever, my great-grandfather on my mother's side, was a native Scotsman. He came to California in the 1850s by way of Canada West. He didn't work in the mines either. He built a hotel in Magalia, hired some Chinese to do the work, and lived the life of a gentleman on the gold dust the miners paid him for a clean bed and wholesome meals. He also had a freight-hauling business and brought goods to the Magalia mines from the valley down below. He did quite well financially and never had a sore back from digging.

My father's name was Willard Agustus. He had a wonderfully kind countenance which reflected his true personality. He was a good and moral man in all of his personal and business dealings. In contrast to my mother's personality, he was easygoing and had a tendency to think good of everyone and to trust each and every person with whom he came in contact.

Mother was the opposite in personality from my father. Her temper was quick. When she was displeased, she left no doubt in anyone's mind about what it was that displeased her. She was a perfectionist, high strung, with a nervous disposition. She was a good moral person and a strict disciplinarian.

My mother, whose full name was Margaret Jane, was known to all of her family and friends as just plain Maggie. My father adored her and would do anything for her. She was an average size woman with jet black hair that had a decided curl to it. From her early twenties there was a one inch white streak in her hair extending from her forehead to the crown of her head. She claimed it was due to a series of violent headaches she had suffered early in her adult life.

In 1892 my mother and father were married. They went to San Francisco and honeymooned at the Palace Hotel. The first morning of their marriage Dad heard mother crying while she was dressing for breakfast. This made Dad feel terrible, thinking he had done something to upset her, so he asked her why she was crying.

It turned out she couldn't do her hair up the way she wanted it. Dad did his best to help her, but having been raised with six brothers and no sisters around the house, he didn't have the foggiest idea what to do to help. They struggled for quite some minutes in a vain attempt to arrange her waist-length hair into a bouffant. Mother finally confessed to her new husband that she had never in her entire life had to comb her own hair. When Dad asked her who in the world had done it for her, she reluctantly acknowledged that her mother had always done up her hair.

Rather than cut their honeymoon short, Father made a quick decision. He took his sobbing bride by the hand to the hotel's barber shop and ordered the barber to cut her hair short enough that she could manage it herself.

According to the family story, Mother cried and carried on the entire time the barber clipped away her hair.

Immediately after the shearing, Dad took Mother to a milliner and bought her a new chapeau. The hats she had brought with her no longer fit. They were designed with extra large crowns to go around the bouffant style of that day.

Dad never tired of spinning this yarn about his beloved Maggie. When he finished this tale, embroidered with numerous little side anecdotes, Mother and Father laughed until they had tears running down their cheeks.

Mother was the driving force behind our family. Once she set her mind to do something, it eventually happened. She worked extremely hard to make ends meet and to make our home comfortable.

Both of my parents were extremely hard-working people who left their parents' home at an early age because they had to find gainful employment. My mother told me she was out working and sending money home to help support her widowed mother while she was still in her early teens. I felt it became an obsession with both of them to work, plan, and contrive methods to give my brother and me a better start in life than they had as youngsters.

3

My Father

Dad was born at home on March 2, 1869, at Central House, California, a small farming district eleven miles south of Oroville. When he was young he had sandy colored hair and very pink skin. After his hair started thinning, his pink scalp was visible through his white hair. He was six feet, two inches tall and very well proportioned. Although he usually weighed 190-195 pounds, he was never what one would consider fat.

Dad began working on his father's farm at the age of twelve. By the time he was fifteen he was doing a man's work. He, like my mother, had only a grammar school education.

For the first nineteen years of his adult life my father labored as a grocery clerk for the firm of Perkins and Wise, the largest wholesale-retail house north of Sacramento. George Perkins went on to become one of the most famous persons to come out of Oroville. He was elected as Republican Governor of California in 1879 and in 1894 was appointed to serve out the remainder of Leland Stanford's term to the United States Senate. He was elected in his own right for a six-year term in 1903.

My father had the most even temperament of anyone I have ever known. One day, when he was very old I mentioned, "You never said a cross word to me that I can remember, and you only spanked me once, when I was about two years old!" He smiled and then said, "You never needed it. You always tried to do what was right.""

The spanking came about in this way. (I was too young to remember it, but I was told the story often enough that it seems as if I do.) Dad, who was in the California militia, was called to active duty at the start of the Spanish-American War. I was only a little over a year old when he left. Mother was lonely and I was too, so, I started sleeping with her. When the war was over and Dad came home, I didn't want to give up my place in Mother's bed to a stranger.

The first night, as fast as Dad could carry me back to my own room, I hopped out of my crib and rejoined them. I guess Dad had other things on his mind which didn't include me. After a number of tries to make me stay in my own bed, Father's frustration finally got the best of him and he laid his hand a number of times on my back side. I got the hint and learned to stay in my own room at night.

Dad was very civic minded. In addition to being a volunteer fireman and a member of the town band, he felt it was his duty to stay in the militia even after his stint in the Spanish-American War.

Willard Agustus Westwood in his Spanish-American War uniform, circa 1897. (Rohrbacher Family Collection)

On April 18, 1906, San Francisco was ravaged by a powerful earthquake and then scorched by an all-consuming fire. My father's militia unit was called up for duty in San Francisco. Their assignment was to assist the victims and stand guard against looting. Dad, who was a corporal, was on duty for several weeks. His unit camped in Golden Gate Park. When he came home, he brought a pair of miniature brass dragons he found in the ashes of a burned out building in Chinatown. For many years these dragons graced our hearth and served as a constant reminder of San Francisco's dreadful catastrophe.

Father was self-taught and took instruction for several years with the International School of Correspondence. He studied his textbooks each night after working a ten-hour day at the grocery store. I can still see him, wearing his horned-rimmed glasses, hunched over the dining room table, pouring over his books while doing his assignments. He set a good example and was a wonderful role model for my brother and me. Eventually he passed his examinations and started a new career as surveyor and assayer with the Hammond Dredger Gold Mining Company.

Each dredger crew cleaned out their gold riffles once a week. Father's job was to go out to the dredgers, gather up the gold mixed with mercury, and tote it to the small shack where he did the retorting.

A typical gold dredger working a pond on the Feather River, circa 1910. *(Courtesy California State Library Collection)*

Retorting is a fancy name for distilling something, in this case mercury. Already in a liquid form, mercury vaporizes at a much lower temperature than that at which gold melts. The mercury was distilled to be used over and over again. During this process the gold and other base metals were left behind.

Part of Father's job was to weigh the gold amalgam before he left the dredger. After the retorting process, the weight of the recovered mercury and gold had to tally. After the gold had been separated from the mercury, it was melted and poured into bricks. Finally, it was taken, under guard, to the Wells Fargo office where it was weighed, certified, and sent, again under guard, to the United States Mint at San Francisco.

Dad was guarded by a sentry with a loaded shotgun. All around the retort shack was a high fence with a locked gate and a large sign with bold letters warning people away. Handling gold carried with it great responsibility and trust. Dad was justifiably proud of the confidence the company had placed in him. The $200 per month he was paid was an excellent salary for 1907. By his own admission, the four years he worked for the Hammond Gold Dredging Company were the happiest working years of his life.

This, however, came to an abrupt end. Father was catapulted back into the grocery business when, under duress, he was induced by his brother John, to leave the best job he had ever had.

Dad's oldest brother, my Uncle John, had loaned $10,000, a small fortune at that time, to a man who owned one of the two grocery stores in town. To all appearances the grocery business was going along just fine until one Monday morning the store failed to open. The man who had borrowed money from Uncle John had skipped the country and left an enormous number of unpaid bills. He had allowed the store's stock to run down to a bare minimum, leaving the shelves stripped and the stockroom empty.

As Grandfather Westwood had already passed on, Uncle John, seventeen years older than my father, was the head of the family. He promptly called an emergency meeting of the clan. He said to my father, "Will, you've got to help me out. You know about grocery stores, and I don't know anything but farming."

The six brothers and Grandma Westwood decided that since Dad had spent many years working in a grocery store and knew the business, it was his duty to come to the assistance of his older brother. It was further decided he should take over the running of the nearly defunct grocery store in an attempt to recover the money his brother had invested in the business. Dad didn't have to make a down payment to his brother, but he did take on the obligation to pay, without interest, Uncle John's original $10,000 investment. Obviously, the outcome of the meeting had been decided long before it was called into session.

This was a major turning point in our household. Father was heartsick at the thought of giving up doing the work he truly loved, but solving a family problem took precedence over an individual's personal wants and desires.

Getting the grocery store back on its feet was uphill going for quite a while. It took every cent my father could scrape together to restock the store and bring the business into the black. On top of everything else, Dad was not the best businessman in the world because he had a soft spot in his heart for any poverty-stricken woman with a brood of children who walked into his store and asked for credit.

Dad brought a young man named Earl Ward into the business. Mr. Ward had worked as a grocery clerk all of his life. Eventually Dad made Mr. Ward a full partner. The store was first known as W. A. Westwood, Grocer, then later as Westwood and Ward, Grocers.

The business was located on the southwest corner of Montgomery and Lincoln Streets until the lease on the building ran out in 1914. Henry Bird, an old family friend, put up a large brick building on the opposite corner of the same street. Dad and Mr. Ward moved their store into new quarters and operated the business there for many years.

By 1914 they were doing both retail and wholesale business and owned a horse barn and a number of delivery wagons. They had the contract for all the wholesale grocery trade for the development of the Western Pacific Railroad in the Feather River Canyon.

The store was on three levels. In the basement or cellar were cases of smoked meats and cheeses and row upon row of oaken barrels full of whisky, brandies, and various kinds of wine. Part of the ground level of the store was for the retail trade. Here, a succession of shelves held canned and bulk groceries. In the rear were enormous piles of sacked grain. These sacks weighed 100 pounds and had to be bucked by hand. The upper floor was for storage of case goods. The three floors were connected by a hydraulic elevator.

The Myers Street entrance, where the loading dock was located, was always congested with wagons of all sizes waiting to be loaded or unloaded. They ranged from two-horse teams pulling a simple buckboard to enormous outfits with a dozen or more horses or mules and driven by a jerk-line. They carried supplies for the mines, small stores, hotels, farms, and for the crews who manned the gold dredgers. They also brought in goods from the valley or from the railroad station.

At its peak the store had a total of twenty-seven full-time clerks and drivers plus two girls doing clerical work and taking phone orders. I still remember the phone number of the store: it was "One."

Practically all the orders came in over the telephone. Staples such as flour, rice, sugar, coffee, beans and so forth had to be cut, measured or weighed, and wrapped because there were very few packaged foods on the market. Father's store handled no fruits or vegetables except potatoes, oranges and apples. These were sold by the bushel basket or in 100-pound sacks. When available, bananas were stocked but were only sold by the bunch. The store did a big business in sacks of grain, oats, and bales of hay which were stored at the horse barn.

The clerks filled the orders, boxed, and loaded them aboard buckboards to be delivered. Two deliveries a day were made to each section of the town, one in the morning for orders called in the day before and an afternoon delivery for orders received before noon. The groceries were brought to the door of the customer, carried into her kitchen, and deposited on the kitchen table.

The girls were very busy as practically every customer ran a charge account and had to be billed at the end of the month. When a woman called to order anything of an intimate nature, there was a well understood code word for it. For example, one never asked for toilet paper. Instead they said, "Please send me six packages of T.P."

The men worked long hours. My father reported in at seven o'clock in the morning and worked until seven in the evening five days a week. On Saturdays the stores remained open until nine in the evening. My brother and I only had the opportunity to get acquainted with our father on Sundays and holidays, when the store was closed.

Dad's wholesale business serviced the little stores and hotels up the Feather River canyon. Earlier, until the track laying, tunnel drilling and bridge building on the Feather River project was finished, he did a great deal of business with the concessionaires who ran the commissaries that fed the railroad workers. These orders were sent out each day on the Western Pacific Railroad work trains.

I learned a great deal about the inner workings of my father's business. The entire time I was in high school and at the University I worked in the office during my summer vacations while each of the girls took her month's vacation with pay. Everyone who worked for Father received the same pay—clerks, drivers and the office girls. Each earned seventy-five dollars a month.

4

Duties of the Sexes

Sex was a term never used in polite society. I never heard the word spoken aloud until 1914 after I had enrolled at the University of California. Its only application then was in a zoology or biology class for purposes of identification.

The duties of the sexes were pretty clearly defined. Women did not cut lawns, paint fences, build things, prune trees, or clean out the chicken yard. Mother never learned nor had the occasion or inclination to use a wrench, screwdriver, or hammer.

Women were expected to keep a clean and tidy home, produce children, wash, iron, mend, knit, sew, and set a decent table. The old saying, "Man, he works from sun to sun; a woman's work is never done," was more than true. At that time there was a clear-cut division of labor.

The woman of the house was expected to run her home, and the man was expected to furnish the money for the household expenses. It was the woman's responsibility to make the money stretch until the end of the month. If she was a good manager and economized by husbanding her resources and practicing good organization, she might end the month with a surplus of cash. In the eyes of most husbands that money was hers and could be used for her special needs. Woe be it to a housewife who consistently failed to make her household money stretch until the last day of the month and had to ask her husband for an additional allotment.

There was so much cooking, sewing, ironing and washing to do to keep her family looking presentable that most women had little time for frivolity.

We had chickens which produced enough meat and eggs to supply our family's needs. In addition to chickens we had a large vegetable garden, rows of berry vines and a strawberry patch. Except for the heavy spade work at planting time, the care of the garden was the women's responsibility.

During harvest time, the women canned several varieties of fruits and vegetables. They also made jams, jellies, preserves, and put up a few lugs of tomatoes. We even made our own catsup. All this was designed to get us through the winter when produce was unavailable.

Women who had to work away from the home, except for teachers and trained nurses, were usually objects of pity. In most cases, they worked as clerks in the dry goods stores, labored as domestics, or were telephone operators. The majority of these women were either spinsters, widows, or had been deserted by their husbands.

Summer and winter, all cooking was done on a wood burning stove. The men took care of cutting and splitting the firewood, bringing it into the kitchen and stacking it. Their kitchen chores ended there except when chickens were to be killed and plucked. That was a man's job.

The way things were done wasn't always a happy solution to a full life for either of the sexes, but that's the way things were done at the dawn of the twentieth century.

5

Domestic Work Week

MONDAY

Rain or shine, unless it fell on Christmas or New Year's, this day was set aside as wash day. Our wash was usually hung on permanent lines in the back yard. If it rained, we had permanent hooks on the porches from which lines were strung for clothes to be hung out to dry. Clothes were hung to dry on the porches on every side of the house except the front porch. People felt hanging laundry on the front porch was untidy and rather slovenly.

Over the stove hung a wooden rack which was suspended from clotheslines on pulleys. This rack could be lowered to be loaded with small or thick items of wash that needed heat to dry. Once it was loaded with freshly laundered articles, it was hoisted close to the ceiling where the heat from the stove quickly dried the items. This was used for articles that had to be ready to be ironed the next day.

Wash day began on Sunday night. The call went out after our Sunday supper for everyone to empty their wicker hampers and bring the dirty clothing to the back porch for sorting. Everything was separated into piles of dirty clothes. The whites in one stack and colored items in another. Bath towels and sheets were lumped into separate batches.

After the sorting process the soiled laundry was dumped into the wash tubs to soak over night. This job had to be finished before we were allowed to retire on Sunday night.

Washing was a terrific job that started at the crack of dawn. It was essential to get a head start on the day's task before it was time to prepare breakfast for the family. Many hours of back-breaking work would take place before the task was finished. It was, to say the least, damned hard work and very labor intensive, requiring strong backs and many willing female hands.

We didn't have the convenience of soap powder, so a cake of yellow laundry soap was grated into a pot of boiling water. Once it had melted, the mixture was doled out into wash tubs full of hot water. The tubs were large, round, and made of galvanized iron with handles on the side. Between uses they were nested in a stack on the back porch.

Every woman in the family pitched in on wash day to help. There was a lot to be done, such as scrubbing, wringing, rinsing, starching, poking at the clothing in the boiler with a broom stick, packing hot water to the tubs on the back porch, emptying used water and then refilling the tubs, and finally, pegging the clothes in an orderly fashion on the lines. Many hands made the labor go much faster.

The first assignment of the day was to select out of the soak water the hand laundry such as shirts, blouses, underwear, socks, handkerchiefs, table napkins and pillow cases and scrub them on the washboard. Larger pieces such as table cloths and sheets were washed by hand in the soapy soak water.

Once things had been inspected by Grandmother or Mother and considered ready, anything that was white—sheets, table linen, shirts, underwear, handkerchiefs, and such were boiled in clear water, rinsed twice, and then put to soak in water laced with a generous amount of bluing. After each soaking the laundry had to be wrung out and deposited in wicker laundry baskets.

We were lucky because in our home we had a hand cranked wringer. One of us had to operate it by turning the crank while someone else fed the laundry through the rubber covered wringers, one item at a time. This was an onerous and burdensome job. By the end of a session of heavy-duty wringing one's shoulders screamed with pain from the exertion. This was especially true because each item as it went through the various rinses had to be run through the wringer three or four times. The families who were not lucky enough to have a wringer were forced to twist each item until most of the water had been squeezed out of the material. Large pieces took strong hands and arms. Because of their size, sheets and table cloths were especially formidable, and it took two people to do a halfway creditable wringing job.

Finally, all of the items that needed to be starched were run through a tub in which a thick solution of boiled starch had been prepared. Two consistencies of starch were concocted, one light and one heavy.

The objective was to have everything washed, rinsed, wrung out, and ready to hang out by the time I was ready to leave for school at eight-thirty that morning.

If a woman wanted to maintain her self respect in the neighborhood, she had to finish hanging out her last piece of laundry by ten. In our home ten o'clock was not acceptable. My mother and grandmother tried to get everything pegged onto the line by shortly after nine.

There was a certain amount of logic in our women folk's compulsive drive to meet their self-imposed nine o'clock deadline. In this way the ladies could allow themselves the luxury of a few moments to sit down, put their feet up, and drink a cup of tea before it was time to start the noon meal, or dinner as we called it in those days.

The noon meal on Monday was a boiled dinner. On wash day, dinner was served at twelve noon, the same as on any other day. The boiled dinner was very practical. This was a meal which required very little watching while cooking. Even during the hottest months the stove had to go full blast all morning to furnish boiling water for the wash. That meant there was enough hot water and heat in the stove to boil a good-sized chunk of meat. When it was tender all my mother or grandmother had to do was add vegetables, shove the pot to the back of the stove, and wait for noon when everyone came trooping in expecting a good meal. My father came home from work for his dinner as did my brother and I.

As soon as the laundry was dry enough to take down from the line, everything was brought into the kitchen, dampened, rolled tightly, and packed into laundry baskets, ready for Tuesday's ironing. No woman who valued her self-respect and standing in the neighborhood let her laundry hang outdoors over night. If the chore of sprinkling and rolling the laundry couldn't be finished before supper, it was completed immediately after the dishes were washed and put away.

TUESDAY

This day was much harder than wash day. But there were certain payoffs which made it much more interesting and in some ways easier to deal with.

The first task was to build a roaring fire in the stove. The wood supply had to be sufficient to keep the fires going at high heat beneath all burners all day. Before bedtime on Monday, the men went to the wood shed to split firewood and stacked it in the kitchen next to the stove.

Our flatirons were made of heavy cast iron. The only way to heat them was to place them on the wood burning stove. It took a minimum of four of these heavy irons to do the job. Our irons were mostly of the patented type. These had wooden handles that clipped onto the base. We also had some of the older models that had permanently attached wooden handles. The patented type were an advantage over the old models. While the base was heating, the handles of the old models became intensely hot from being on the stove. The clip-on handles stayed cool.

Ironing began immediately after the breakfast table was cleared. As soon as the ironing board was set up and the irons had come up to a high enough temperature to do the job, work began. The correct temperature was determined by a drop of spit on the end of a person's finger touched gingerly and quickly to the face of the iron. If it hissed or sizzled, it was time to go to work. If you were using one of the old irons, it was necessary to hold it with a pot holder until the handle was cool enough to touch with your bare hands. The iron was used until it cooled down so much it no longer did the job. It was then returned to the stove and exchanged for a hot one and so on until the last piece of ironing was finished.

I was ten years old when I was integrated into the Tuesday ironing chores. Although she loved to read, Grandmother's eyesight was poor. She especially liked serialized stories from magazines. My usual assignment was to sit by the ironing board with my back to the light and read aloud one or more of the serials out of such magazines as the *Ladies Home Journal* and *Good Housekeeping*. On some Tuesdays I read a couple of chapters from whatever novel Grandmother happened to be reading at the moment.

The piles of ironing we had to work through in those days was immense. The fancy work for both men and women was starched and needed careful treatment. The cuffs, collars, and fronts of men's everyday or work shirts were done at home. Dress shirts with their stiff fronts and detachable collars were sent to the Chinese laundry on Broderick Street. Some families used the Oroville Steam Laundry on High Street which also did things up beautifully.

Sheets, pillowcases, tablecloths, napkins, bureau scarves, and linen towels had to be hand ironed and carefully folded. Mother insisted that everything of one kind had to be folded in exactly the same way so they would stack neatly in the linen closet or the bureau drawer. The final task of the day was to put all of the freshly ironed things away. They had to be placed in the appropriate place in the linen closet at the bottom of the stack. In this way they could have a rest before it was their turn to be used again. Mother was most particular about this, and more than once I had to unload an entire linen shelf and reload it because the stack was not up to her standard of neatness.

We had one ironing board so only one person could iron at a time. The person who wasn't pushing the iron at the moment spent her "resting" time baking cakes or pies, making bread, or roasting a joint of meat. This was a very practical thing to do, as the oven was hot and might as well be put to use. Tuesday dinner was a special feast.

If, by the time I came home from school, the ironing wasn't finished, provided I wasn't pressed into reading aloud, I was given the assignment of doing the table napkins and handkerchiefs. Once I had reached the age of menstruation, this was the time for me to do up my bundle of sanitary napkins. Mother or Grandmother stood guard to make sure my brother, his friends, or a boy cousin didn't burst into the kitchen while I was taking care of this monthly chore. I assume Mother took care of hers while we were in school because I never saw her ironing her own sanitary supplies.

If in the opinion of either of the women of the house I had done a sloppy ironing job, the items were promptly redampened and I was ordered to do them again. I must have been forced to do a good number of them over, because to this day, I still hate the thought of ironing.

WEDNESDAY

Grandmother and Mother, after their strenuous Monday and Tuesday, took Wednesday as their day of rest. That afternoon they either went to a tea party, sewing bee, or to the Ladies Aid Society. They left the house immediately after dinner and wouldn't come home until just before supper was due to be served. On the Wednesdays they didn't go out, they invited company to their home.

When they arrived home they were usually in a rush to get things together to feed the family. The first thing they did was take off their coats and hats and slip into their work aprons to begin our supper. This was usually a cold meal which had been prepared before they left for their afternoon's outing. My job was to set the table.

Some Wednesdays they invited their lady friends in for tea and cake which was served on our best chinaware. They also enjoyed doing intricate needlepoint or embroidery. Many times the ladies prepared a layette for a new baby. This usually included a complete set of clothes, booties, bedding, and diapers. Occasionally they worked on a special quilt for a church bazaar raffle. Sometimes it was to be given as a present to a very particular friend of the sewing circle who was ill or celebrating an anniversary.

When we arrived home from school, Bill was usually asked to play the piano to entertain the ladies. I was asked to recite the latest dramatic piece I had committed to memory. The visitors' remarks were kind and their response indicated they were appreciative of our efforts.

After we had finished amusing the ladies, my brother and I were given the opportunity to enjoy the refreshments. In hot months we had ice cold lemonade instead of tea or milk.

On special occasions Mother served her guests a punch made from lemon and orange juice, claret wine, and sizzle water. The punch and a large chunk of ice were placed in a cut glass punch bowl and served in matching cut glass cups.

THURSDAY and FRIDAY

Thursday and Friday were not very special days. The men went to work as usual at eight in the morning and came home only to eat their noon meal until after the store had closed. Men worked a straight fifty-plus-hour work week with no extra pay for overtime. For them, each workday was much like the one before.

For the women, these two days were usually set aside for such practical things as sewing, mending, and darning socks. The trusty treadle Singer sewing machine in the dining room was opened, and Mother and Grandmother caught up on their sewing. This consisted of either making clothing for the family, repairing items, or working on some project for the house such as drapes, new curtains, bed or table linen, or numerous other projects.

SATURDAY

Saturdays were different because we worked without letup from the time we got out of bed until after supper that evening. This day seemed much harder because so many of the chores were assigned to me.

We cleaned the house from top to bottom. The first job of the day was to take down at least one set of lace curtains and wash, starch, and stretch them on the pins of the adjustable curtain stretcher. This was the first job of the day to ensure the curtains would be dry in time to rehang them that same day. Windows were washed with ammonia water and polished with crumpled up newspapers.

All the beds in the house were changed. This consisted of stripping the pillow cases from all the pillows and replacing them with fresh ones. Then the top sheet was moved to the bottom and a crisp, clean sheet put on top. My job was to follow after Mother and Grandmother to collect soiled sheets and put them in the laundry hamper.

Because we didn't have an electric vacuum cleaner, we cleaned the rugs in another way. We saved newspapers all week for the Saturday cleaning. Newspapers were soaked in a bucket of warm water, squeezed out, and then torn into bits about the size of a playing card. The scraps of damp paper were spread all over the carpets. My job was to walk over every inch of the carpet to press the wet scraps into the nap of the rug. Mother or Grandmother followed after me and swept up the paper. This not only picked up the lint and dirt, but it kept the dust down.

After the bed-making and sweeping it was time to dust the furniture and rub it with polish. My job was to get down on my knees and polish the rungs and legs of the chairs and the lower portions of the tables.

When the furniture polishing was finished, it was time to tidy our bureau drawers. The shelves in the kitchen and pantry were then washed and straightened. Every square inch of the kitchen floor was scrubbed on hands and knees.

When all assigned tasks were completed to Mother's satisfaction, it was time to take our Saturday night baths, wash our hair, and get ready to go to town for our Saturday evening outing and to shop and meet the men-folk.

All of this was done each week in addition to our usual spring cleaning which took an entire week sometime during the forty days of Lent. My girl friends and I used to refer to spring cleaning as "Hell Week."

A Chinese man was hired for the week to help with the heavy work. Every carpet was taken up, stretched over the clothes line and given a thorough beating. Every lace curtain in the house was washed, starched, stretched until dry, and then rehung. Any painting or paper hanging that needed attention was taken care of.

All of the kitchen cupboards were emptied and every piece of good chinaware and glassware was washed, polished, and put away on freshly papered shelves. All silver and brass in the house was polished to a bright and sparkling finish. The entire family lived in a decontaminated, Lysol- and pine-scented Hades until Mother and Grandmother declared spring cleaning to be at an end.

In my mother's home, there was a place for everything and everything was kept in its proper place, or else! She kept a feather duster at the sitting room door, and before we set foot in the house, we had to dust off our shoes. I was mortified to have to caution my friends to use the feather duster on their shoes before they entered our home. My friends were aware of my mother's reputation for keeping a clean house and took it in their stride.

In the winter months if the weather was wet, we wore rubber overshoes and took them off on the porch along with our shoes. If there had been an unexpected rain storm and we were caught without our overshoes, we were expected to scrape our shoes clean and then take them off before venturing one step into the house. During the winter months carpet slippers were kept by the door for us to wear inside. Father, winter or summer, took off his shoes and put on carpet slippers before coming into the house.

My mother and everyone else in her family were particularly good housekeepers. I think they were almost compulsive about it. I believe she gloried in having and maintaining that reputation among her friends.

Mother's housekeeping was not limited to the inside of the house. The walks were swept daily, and there wasn't a weed to be seen in the flower or vegetable gardens. In the fall, a leaf could barely alight on the ground before it was raked and deposited in the mulch pile.

SUNDAY

We arose fairly early and had a big breakfast. The entire family went to St. John's Episcopal Church on Second Avenue for the eleven o'clock service.

This day was truly looked upon as a day of rest and relaxation. Even sewing was not allowed. If we sewed on Sunday, we were told we would have to pick out the stitches with our noses before we could enter into the Kingdom of Heaven. Mother never allowed us to do homework on Sunday. We were expected to have that sort of thing out of the way on Friday afternoon or sometime Saturday.

I never quite figured out how cooking, sorting laundry, and other household duties were okay on Sunday, but sewing and homework weren't. It had something to do with what was considered to be absolutely necessary and what wasn't.

We children found the Sunday afternoons and evenings rather dull.

6

Food

Most homes had a basement or cellar where smoked hams and bacon were hung from the rafters. On the floor of the cellars were crocks filled with all sorts of pickles—sweet, sour, salt, dill, sliced bread and butter, and peach. The walls were lined with shelves containing row after row of preserve glasses filled with jelly, jams and marmalade. Chowchow (mixed pickles) and tomato relish were put up in Kerr quart jars. A whole section was given over to canned tomatoes, onion and green peppers. The rest were plain stewed tomatoes. The fruit section was a mixture of quart and half-gallon jars of pears, apricots, cherries, pickled grapes, peaches and apple sauce.

Each year, during the canning season, the previous season's jars were transferred to the front of the shelves and the new ones stored at the back. We seldom had to buy fruit for canning or jam as our farmer uncles brought us all we could use.

At that time of the year every woman in the family pitched in to wash and boil jars, peel and put up the fruit. We worked many days from the crack of dawn to as late as eleven or twelve at night to get the job done.

The entire house was filled with the delightful aroma of whatever happened to be in the process of being preserved that day. Unless you have smelled a dishpan full of piccalilli simmering at the back of the stove, you have missed one of the most elegant aromas in all this world. Catsup in the making is nearly as good.

On baking day pies and three- and four-layer cakes along with their special serving plates and flat silver were displayed on the sideboard so the entire family could admire them.

I loved the delightful sensation of walking into our home to the fragrance of hot raised rolls and fresh baked bread. There is nothing quite as pleasant as the smell of baker's yeast permeating an entire house. All of these gorgeous smells blended with the aroma of baking pies, cakes, and a variety of cookies.

Before we had a telephone, when we came home from school, Mother made out a grocery list, and gave it to my brother Bill or me to take downtown to the grocery store to be filled. The order was delivered to our home the next morning. After we handed over the grocery list, Mother usually had us stop at the butcher shop to pick up some meat. This was a very special chore because the butcher usually gave us a large slice of bologna to eat on the way home and a bone or two for our dog, Fred. Mother, being a frugal person, often put the dog bones into the soup kettle before Fred had an opportunity to gnaw on them.

The milkman came so early in the morning that we seldom saw him except once a month when he collected. Our daily two quarts were measured out from one of the big cans on his milk wagon. If we wanted whipping cream, we put a covered pint jar beside the pan. The cream was thick enough to be spooned out in great heaping gobs.

I would guess that my mother, according to today's standards, knew nothing about nutrition. She may have read a few articles in the *Ladies Home Journal* or *Good Housekeeping* along with each magazine's monthly recipes, but I am sure she knew nothing at all about food values or the basic food groups. Calories, vitamins, and cholesterol were unheard of by the average homemaker. Despite her lack of nutritional knowledge, Mother managed to feed us a well-balanced diet. Wonderful bread stuff—including biscuits, muffins, pancakes, cornbread—was served at every meal. Copious quantities of vegetables plus fresh or canned fruit kept our bowels open while meat gave us strong muscles and healthy red blood. Condiments, relish and desserts were purely for the pleasure of the palate. Dessert was a part of every meal—provided you ate all of your other food first.

Dinner was always the big meal of the day and was ready, come hell or high water, at exactly twelve noon on the dot. It usually consisted of meat, potatoes, and vegetables as the backbone of the meal. On Fridays some kind of fish was substituted for meat. We never had salads except on Sunday when we often had canned shrimp or crab salad. In place of a salad, there was either a bowl of freshly made coleslaw, sliced tomatoes, cucumbers, red onions in vinegar, cottage cheese, or a big platter of wilted lettuce. Dessert was most often some variety of pie.

Supper was typically made from leftovers. We often had hash, stuffed peppers, chili beans, macaroni made with left over pot roast and gravy mixed with canned tomatoes and topped with grated soft cheese. Split pea soup normally followed a leg of lamb dinner. Bubble and squeak—minced meat and vegetables fried together until they squeak—followed corned beef and cabbage. When there weren't enough leftovers to make a meal, we had something like oyster stew or clam chowder or an ersatz kind of chop suey made from ham or bacon and vegetables served over rice. Dessert was usually canned fruit with cake or cookies.

At both dinner and supper there was a big stack of homemade bread and a generous supply of fresh churned butter on the table. A large pot of strong black tea with sugar and cream was also served at both the noon and evening meals.

Sunday morning breakfast featured dried, salt or smoked fish. It could be anything from kippered herring to cod. We had salmon when it was in season. Kippers were served plain with scrambled, fried, or poached eggs. Fresh caught fish or cod was usually served in a milk gravy with potatoes boiled in their jackets, and hot biscuits. Sunday breakfast, an English custom brought from the old country by my grandparents, was served at eight o'clock. Before breakfast Father usually killed and plucked two or three chickens for dinner. While Dad was busy with the chickens, Mother made custard for the ice cream. The chickens and the custard were placed in the cellar to cool until after church. We would hand churn the ice cream just before it was time to sit down for dinner.

Sunday dinner was the most festive meal of the week and was served at two o'clock. More often than not, we had company for this meal. We usually had fried chicken and pan gravy with either a crab or shrimp salad, mashed potatoes, and vegetables. Dessert was some variety of layer cake accompanied by our home-made ice cream slathered with the custard Mother had prepared earlier. The table was set with our best chinaware, glassware, silverware, and table linen.

There was no formal supper on Sunday. The food was usually cold and made up of leftovers from the noon meal. Occasionally Dad went to a downtown restaurant and brought home an oyster loaf wrapped in layers of newspaper to keep it hot. A loaf consisted of an unsliced loaf of bread with the top cut off and the bread between the crusts scooped out. The cavity was filled with breaded, fried oysters. The lid was put back on the loaf and baked in a hot oven for a short time. This allowed the luscious juices from the oysters to soak into the bread. Dad served it by slicing the loaf into equal portions.

On other occasions Dad brought home steamed tamales. They were the big round type in which generous amounts of chicken, beef, or pork was combined with a thick red tamale sauce. The filling was wrapped in layer upon layer of dried corn husks. Between each of the husks a thin layer of cooked corn meal was spread. The round, plump tamales, tied at each end with string, were popped into a steamer to cook. They were a rare treat as they were quite expensive. Each cost fifteen or twenty cents. One tamale with French bread and a tossed green salad was a complete meal for an adult.

Except in the dead of winter, no hot tea or coffee was served at Sunday supper as the kitchen stove was allowed to go out after Sunday's dinner had been served.

On weekdays and Saturdays breakfast was served at six-fifteen sharp. In cold weather porridge with cream and sugar was the first course. Next came ham or bacon, eggs, hot biscuits with pan gravy, pancakes with syrup, or muffins with a choice of jam or jelly. Fresh ground coffee was brewed and served with cream and sugar.

On Saturday mornings we ate baked beans and brown bread. Grandmother prepared them on Friday using her special recipe. She boiled navy beans until they were a certain tenderness; then she spooned them into a big brown bean pot and mixed them with chunks of salt pork, onions, mustard, and a generous amount of black strap molasses.

The noon meal on Mondays was a boiled dinner such as corned beef and cabbage, or boiled flank with carrots, potatoes, parsnips, and fresh corn when it was in season.

Monday night's supper was made up from the leftovers from the noon meal. The usual fare was sliced meat, hash, or bubble and squeak.

Summer Monday evening meals were hard to beat. The entree was usually a platter of some type of cold sliced meat, served with chowchow or piccalilli. Another platter held sliced tomatoes and cucumbers. There was a supply of home-baked bread with copious amounts of butter. The meal was followed by canned peaches or pears for dessert.

Friday we ate fish. Roman Catholics were obligated to eat meatless meals on Friday. Those of us who were not Catholic ate fish because that was the only day fresh fish was available.

We didn't have garbage. What we didn't or couldn't eat was fed to the dog or the chickens. If it was good enough for the family, it was good enough for them. Fred ate everything we did from wilted lettuce to canned peaches. His diet must have agreed with him as he lived fourteen years.

Anything that couldn't be burned in the stove or fireplace or worked into the mulch pile became trash. This included broken glass or china, tin foil, empty bottles, tin cans, pieces of metal like garter fasteners, and broken buttons. These things went into a gunny sack which hung in the cellar. When it was full, Father took it out to the city dump.

Potato peelings, vegetable trimmings, and ashes from the stove and fireplace went into the mulch pile. To this was added grass clippings, fallen leaves, and chicken droppings. With a good mulch pile at our disposal, there was no need to waste good money on fertilizer for our vegetable and flower gardens.

7

The Farm

Some of the happiest days of my youth were spent at the farm because I loved my cousins and I adored Grandma. Life on the farm was so very different from life in town. Since there was no electricity, any light in the house after the sun set came from lanterns and candles. One of my daily chores was to help my girl cousins polish the inside of the lamp chimneys with tissue paper. Then we carefully trimmed the lamp wicks and put fresh candles in the candle holders.

Another great difference from town life was the fact that there was no running water in the house. Our only source of water was a hand pump over the kitchen sink. All water for washing dishes, for example, had to be pumped into a bucket and then transferred to a kettle on the stove to be heated. This was also true for hot water for the men to wash and shave in the morning and for the women's needs for wash water. Before retiring in the evening a large container of water was filled and placed on the back of the stove. There was enough heat left in the stove to warm the water during the night.

When the men got up to do their chores, they stoked up the fire and put another pot of water on to heat to make coffee and wash the breakfast dishes.

There were many other differences between the farm and the city, such as caring for the sheep, pigs, horses, and cows. My chores included feeding the animals, cleaning their stalls, and milking the cows. It was a special treat to ride one of the horses. I ran around barefooted with my cousins which I was never allowed to do at home.

I can still see the look on Grandpa Westwood and Uncle John's faces the day the barn burned down. Hay barns in which stock were kept had problems with infestations of fleas and rodents. About once or twice a year, especially before the new mown hay was brought into the barn for winter storage, the place needed to be fumigated. This was accomplished by first raking the loose hay into a pile in the center of the barn's dirt floor. Next the pile of hay was thoroughly wet down. Then Grandpa took some dry straw and built a small fire deep within the pile of wet hay. After that the barn was closed as tightly as possible. It remained closed the entire time the wet hay smoldered. The entire barn was filled with heavy smoke which killed the fleas and anything else that might be infesting the stable. After a couple of hours the smoldering straw exhausted the available oxygen in the barn and burned itself out. The ashes were raked into the barnyard, and the new hay could then be hauled up into the hay loft for winter storage.

One day Uncle John evidently forgot to tell one of the hired hands what was happening. He needed something in the barn and threw open the big double doors, allowing fresh air to rush in. The additional oxygen fanned the smoldering hay into a roaring fire, and in an instant the structure was on fire. The wooden building burned to the ground.

Grandpa and Uncle John never lived it down. Their friends used to kid them about being so desperate to get rid of the fleas and mice that they burned their barn down.

Despite their teasing, Uncle John's neighbors turned up the next week to help him put up a new barn. All it cost was the price of the lumber and enough food to feed the fifteen or twenty men who participated in the two or three days it took for the barn raising.

My fondest memory of the farm was the time I spent in the kitchen with Grandma. She encouraged my girl cousins and me to help with the cooking. She was an excellent teacher and many of her cooking lessons stood me in good stead throughout my life. We made pies, creamed butter and sugar for cakes, skimmed cream off the milk pans, churned butter, grated coconut for cake frosting, ground coffee, popped corn, and generally busied ourselves in her kitchen. I was never permitted to do this at home because Mother and Grandmother felt I would make a mess of their kitchen. Even washing dishes at Grandma's big enameled cast iron sink seemed more like fun than work.

During the day my two girl cousins and I often hitched up the cart and took cool drinking water to the men working in the fields. On weekdays we were allowed to drive the cart the two-mile round trip to the mail drop to pick up the newspaper and our mail.

At night, after Grandpa and Uncle John finished reading the paper, we all gathered around the pump organ. Grandma played hymns while we sang until bedtime.

On Sunday we went to church at the schoolhouse which was five miles away. Grandpa hitched up the surrey, which was big enough for the whole family. On this occasion Grandpa rode instead of walking alongside the horse. I suppose it was because he was wearing his Sunday best clothes and freshly shined shoes and wanted to keep himself as clean as possible.

The visiting Episcopal priest only came out to the country once a month to celebrate a communion service. On the other Sundays, Grandpa conducted Morning Prayer services in his rich English Midland accent. Grandfather wasn't an ordained lay preacher and was not allowed to preach, but he didn't hesitate to make comments and give explanations as he read the Propers on those Sundays.

After church was the time for the farm families to visit. The ladies served fresh brewed coffee, tea, and cakes while the men stood around discussing the weather, politics, farm business, or anything that interested them. Sundays were the time the women folk decided at whose farm everyone would visit the following Wednesday.

For the Wednesday visits we left immediately after breakfast in Grandma's patent leather, upholstered phaeton. We dressed up for these occasions. Grandma was always in her best dress. After Grandpa died, she always dressed in black. The severity of the black was broken by white lace trimmed cuffs and collars. She also wore a big white apron, and a black lace cap pinned onto her beautiful white hair.

When you went visiting on the farm, you never brought your own sewing. The polite thing to do was to sew for your hostess. We rolled and hemmed dishtowels, hemstitched linen napkins or tablecloths, made quilt blocks, or did some quilting. I very seldom said anything, but I listened while the women exchanged recipes, sympathized over hardships, and gossiped.

At noon we had dinner with the host family. At about four, when it was time to leave, we were served a very special and elegant tea, a scrumptious spread of cut sandwiches, bread and butter, and little frosted cakes, served with tea and coffee. Everyone made a lovely day of it. When the ladies arrived home they had loads of interesting news and farm chatter to share with their men.

Farm women were close. In case of illness, accident, or death on a neighbor's farm, they dropped everything to go to do what they could for their neighbor.

Harvest at Uncle John's was an experience. It normally took place just before school started. That meant I was usually on hand to do my bit. It was not unusual to have the start of school delayed if the crops were late because of a late spring or a cooler than normal summer.

The crews who brought in the harvest were all neighbors who willingly and out of necessity helped one another. The crews consisted of some twelve to fifteen men. Uncle John and his sons were gone a week at a time during the gathering in of the crops. They never worked for pay. But they knew that the entire group of neighbors would descend on their farm during the harvest to bring in their crops. When they arrived, each man brought his own blankets, toilet articles, and a change of clothes. They slept in the barn and made their beds in the hay.

Because the weather was hot a huge serving table made of planks on saw horses was set up under a large oak tree just behind the kitchen. Oil cloth was spread over the planks for a table cloth. Hundred-pound grain sacks were used for chairs.

Breakfast was served at four in the morning. This meant Grandma was up at three to prepare and then serve a hearty breakfast to the hungry crew. There were platters of ham, beef steak, fried potatoes, eggs, hot biscuits, gravy, coffee, milk, and pies. Each man ate a minimum of four eggs and no platter was left on the table with a scrap of meat on it. At noon they were served a huge dinner consisting of a roast of some variety of meat or mounds of fried chicken, bread and butter, mashed potatoes and gravy, and dessert.

Evenings, they once again packed away a tremendous meal, usually a cold supper. Before they went to bed they were served watermelon which had been chilling in the cool waters of the pump house all day.

While the harvest was in progress, the women cooked all through the day. The praise Grandma received for her meals was music to her ears. Ladies who were mediocre cooks or were stingy with food were talked about throughout the district. The amazing thing is that despite the amount of calories those men packed away, none of them looked the least bit fat. They needed that amount of food to meet the demands of the heavy manual labor of the harvest.

Those five days were a lark for all of us children. We carried drinking water and cold tea to the men in the fields, rode on the hay wagons, and climbed on the sacks of wheat and barley.

After the harvest Grandma collapsed into her bed for an entire day's rest. We girls were left to run the farm while the men were off harvesting someone else's fields. We took care of all the chores around the place, tiptoed around the house and kept our voices down for twenty-four hours in an effort to allow Grandma to rest.

8

Medicine and Hygiene

O roville had only two medical doctors. One was Old Dr. Benjamin, a homeopathic physician who made his rounds with a satchel full of white, pink, and yellow pills. He had learned his skills by working as an apprentice in a doctor's office. The other was Dr. Wilson who had spent two years studying medicine, then took an examination to receive his diploma and a license to practice.

Later a third physician came to our town to practice medicine. Dr. Kusel was a hometown boy who also happened to come from one of the few Jewish families in our community. He arrived back in town fresh out of an Eastern medical school with the latest and most up-to-date thinking in the field of health and hygiene. At first he had a difficult time selling his "new-fangled" ideas to the townspeople. Fortunately for all of us, he was stubborn and didn't give up easily.

The entire landscape on either side of the river was covered with dredger ponds left behind when outfits like the Hammond Gold Dredger Company and others dredged up the bottom land on both sides of the Feather River. When they were through, they left large ugly piles of turned up river rock and huge pools of stagnant water. Dredger ponds provided excellent breeding conditions for mosquitoes, so everyone I knew had chronic malaria.

To control the malaria problem, quinine pills were dished out in daily doses. If taken religiously they helped to control the disease and keep one from having frequent bouts with chills and fever. Unfortunately, most young people, including myself, detested the taste of the stuff and dropped the bitter pill down the privy. Of course, we paid the price for our obstinate folly.

Dr. Kusel's first success was bringing about the spraying of a light film of crude oil on the dredger ponds to kill the mosquito larva. It was not until 1910 that the town fathers finally took Dr. Kusel's advice and bought a supply of oil and hired someone to spray the ponds. In this way they brought the mosquitoes under control and got rid of the worst of the malaria.

After malaria was out of the way, chronic dysentery, typhoid, child bed fever, whooping cough, measles, small-pox, and consumption were left for the physicians to deal with.

When I was seven I had my first vaccination. It was for smallpox. This was considered a very daring and dangerous thing for my parents to allow. A smallpox epidemic was spreading throughout the town and several people had died. My parents, with great trepidation and fear, decided to take a chance and asked the doctor to give the family the dreaded vaccination. They reasoned it was probably better to lose an arm to infection than take the chance of losing a member of the family to smallpox.

While this was going on, Dr. Kusel conducted a one-man campaign against spitting on the streets. This was his attempt to slow down the spread of the wasting disease of tuberculosis.

When he set up practice, the town's drinking water was drawn, unfiltered, from the Feather River, and dysentery, typhoid fever, and other water related diseases ran rampant in Oroville. Dr. Kusel talked the city fathers into filtering and treating the drinking water after it was pumped out of the river. Through this action alone, he gained acceptance with the powers who ran the city.

My father solved our drinking water problem long before Dr. Kusel came to town. While serving with the army during the Spanish-American War, he learned polluted or contaminated water was the cause of many ills. After he was demobilized and came home, he put his new knowledge into practice. Father had a big, galvanized-iron tank with a wooden cover constructed and installed on the roof of our back porch. This was filled with charcoal mixed with sand. There were a series of screens at the outlet. The tank was filled with water to which Dad occasionally added chlorine tablets. A float valve was installed on the inlet in order to keep the tank constantly full of water. A copper pipe led from the bottom of the tank to the kitchen and then into the ice box. Here the copper pipe was coiled and placed under the ice. A small faucet was attached to the end of the pipe where it emerged from under the block of ice. This gave us the double advantage of having clean, ice cold water to drink.

From that time on, we were only allowed to drink the filtered and chlorinated water that came out of the spigot in the ice box. Untreated river water was used exclusively for cooking and bathing. This practice certainly cut down the incidence of dysentery in our family. It also ended the disgusting habit of routinely finding pollywogs, wigglers, or tiny frogs swimming around in one's water glass.

Unlike the older physicians, Dr. Kusel took the trouble to scrub his hands with soap and water in full view of his patients before touching them. People began to take notice of him and his techniques and procedures, and his medical practice began to grow.

His big break came when the Western Pacific Railroad arrived on a big scale in Oroville. Before they would begin work on the Feather River project, the company demanded a hospital to take care of the many men they knew would be injured and maimed while building bridges, laying track, and blasting tunnels along the Feather River Canyon. Western Pacific offered to put up one half of the cost of a hospital provided the city of Oroville put up the other half.

Dr. Kusel headed the campaign to open the first hospital in Butte County. A big, old mansion in the center of town was purchased and the Oroville General Hospital was born. After that, emergency surgery was no longer performed on the patient's kitchen table.

Almost immediately two graduate nurses were brought into the project, and young ladies who had already finished high school were invited to begin their training to become registered nurses. After the hospital was in full operation Dr. Kusel's practice grew so fast that he eventually had to bring in an assistant.

Despite the new hospital, childbirth was still accomplished at home and in most cases under the care of a midwife like Grandma Phoebe. It was considered quite indelicate to have a man doctor attend such a private performance. It was thought to be far more than any modest woman should have to endure along with the pains of labor.

After childbirth a new mother was not allowed to get out of bed for ten days. Once she was up and around, a full two weeks had to elapse before she could even do light housework. It was believed that early activity after childbirth would bring on early, painful, and irrevocable female disorders. Most families had spinster aunties, grandmothers, or unmarried sisters who could come to help out if there was a medical emergency.

The physicians, even young Dr. Kusel, whom she had delivered, had great respect for Grandma's midwifery and her medical skills and judgment. They often called on her for help in difficult situations. She was especially good with patients suffering from pneumonia. Whenever Grandma was called out on a case she packed a satchel full of medicines and another bag with a change of clothing which included a big starched white apron.

Patients with pneumonia, tuberculosis and other communicable diseases, both acute and chronic, along with a host of other ills were still cared for in the home. This meant that all four of the physicians had lucrative practices. An office call cost one dollar while a home visit was two dollars.

When I was eleven, I had my appendix removed. It had ruptured, and whether I would live or die was in doubt for quite some time. I developed peritonitis and had drainage tubes coming out of the incision draining into jars on the floor. I think I worried more about the expense to my parents than I did about my own mortality or the pain and discomfort my affliction was causing me.

I was a patient in the hospital a full month. The nurse who took care of me was on twenty-four hour duty. This cost my parents the unheard of sum of one hundred dollars a month. My nurse slept beside me on a trundle bed which she pulled out from under my bed each night. She held my hand until I was asleep.

Mother came to the hospital each afternoon at one o'clock and stayed until four to give my nurse a chance to go home for a bath and to change into a clean uniform.

During my illness I was a very important person in the eyes of my friends. They brought me all kinds of flowers and gifts. Once I was allowed to eat candy and fancy foods, they kept me well supplied. After I passed the critical stage, my teachers sent my lessons so I could keep up with my classes. During that month in the hospital plus the additional weeks I spent at home recuperating I developed my life-long love for reading. It also kindled my desire to go on to the university with the intention of studying medicine.

Every family I knew of had a least one tubercular patient to care for in their home. We had two such cases. Fortunately they were not at the same time. The first was cousin Lil who died when she was twenty-four from slow consumption. The second was my mother's younger half-brother Rob who had quick consumption and died when only nineteen years old. He came to live with us so that Mother and Grandmother could take care of him.

Rob's clothes and bedding were washed in Lysol water, then boiled separately from the family's wash. His dishes and cutlery were also kept separate. When he coughed and spit up, he used small squares of torn muslin which he put into a paper bag that was eventually burned in the stove. Anything Rob came in contact with was taboo for us children to handle. We were not allowed to touch him, nor would he allow us to do so. This was very difficult for us because we loved him so dearly. It was a heartbreaking process indeed to watch my lovely young uncle waste away and die.

Down the street from us was another case of quick consumption. This was a youth Rob's age. The two young fellows spent many hours each day together. They believed that rest, wholesome food, and sunshine might cure them. Almost to the end they were hopeful they might recover.

Another small but important health-related item was toilet paper. What we buy in rolls and now take for granted was not in use at that time. What families did to fill the need was to make their own. Tissue paper sewing patterns were saved and cut into good sized squares and kept in a box on a shelf next to the toilet. The first commercial toilet paper came stacked in packages rather than in rolls.

Our family used toothbrushes and tooth powder regularly and also made frequent visits to the dentist. A great many people didn't, however. Because of this, there was a great deal of bad breath, scummy teeth, and toothlessness.

If the dentist found a cavity and needed to drill it out, he used a slow speed drill powered by the dentist or his assistant pumping a food pedal. We didn't have the luxury of novocaine to block the pain.

Once the cavity was drilled out, the dentist filled the hole with either silver amalgam or leaf gold. If he decided to use gold, he utilized a tiny hammer, a miniature metal punch, and small sheets of thin gold. He put layer after layer of gold into the hole and then pounded it into place with the hammer and punch. The soft malleable metal shaped itself to fit the drilled out cavity in the tooth. This wasn't a very pleasant procedure to undergo. On the plus side, this type of gold filling usually lasted for many years, sometimes for life.

Most dentists preferred to pull a tooth instead of trying to save it. A majority of people I knew had false teeth by the time they had reached their forties.

If a woman became ill, she was well cared for. If there were no other women in her home, her needs were attended to by her neighbors. Everyone pitched in and willingly took their turn at working around the patient's home or tending to her assigned nursing duties. If the woman was a widow or spinster lady, husbands and sons of the helpers were pressed into service for such needs as splitting kindling for the stove, patching a leak in the roof, or making any other necessary repairs needed to keep the house liveable.

We may not have been quite as healthy and well cared for medically in those days as we are today, but no one can deny the fact that families and neighbors were close-knit. There certainly was a willingness to step in and help one's neighbor when the need was there.

9

Family Hygiene

In addition to our weekly tub bath, we all took a nightly sponge bath from a wash basin with cold running water located in each bedroom.

My grandmother truly believed that personal cleanliness was next to godliness and acted on that belief with a great deal of enthusiasm bordering on zeal. Much to my chagrin and embarrassment, until I was fourteen, she sponge bathed me every night before bedtime. She, in her words, "washed up as far as possible, down as far as possible," then handed me the wash cloth so I could wash the "impossible."

She also sponge bathed my brother Bill until he set up such a loud howl of protest she had to give it up. Even after he did his own washing, she waited until he was into his night shirt to inspect his neck, ears, hands, and feet.

Foot washing required performing a delicate balancing act. The nightly ritual went like this. We stood with one foot on the floor and one in the basin while she washed that foot. When the foot was deemed clean enough to pass Grandmother's inspection, we hopped around while she dried it. Then we repeated the process with the other foot.

Ladies perspired and men sweated. Without deodorizers, we were all a bit gamey during the summer months despite the fact we used talcum powder and toilet water very lavishly.

Tampons, maxi and mini pads were unheard of. If they had existed, they wouldn't have been mentioned in polite society or advertised. When a girl's breasts started to develop, it was time for her mother to begin preparations for the coming event of menstruation.

In my case, arrangements consisted of the following: First my Grandmother made me an elastic belt with a tab in the front and back to which safety pins were attached. Next a stack of Birdseye diapers were purchased, and I was instructed how to fold them in a special way to form a pad. These articles were assembled into a neat package, wrapped with brown paper and tied with string. Once this was accomplished and the ladies of the house agreed that everything was in readiness, the entire package was squirreled away in the bottom drawer of my bureau. With the handing over of the package came a formidable warning from Mother, underscored by Grandmother, to refrain from discussing these arrangements with anyone, even with my best friend.

I was solemnly warned, at "that time of the month," against exercising, becoming chilled, bathing, or swimming for as long as that part of my cycle lasted. It was felt that any of the just mentioned activities might stop the flow and ultimately cause grave female trouble. No one ever quite explained exactly what was meant by "female troubles." From the sincere tone of the heartfelt advice of my mother and grandmother I was convinced that "female troubles" were the worst thing that could possibly happen to a member of the distaff half of the population. No wonder this truly female occurrence was called "The Curse."

The laundering of these disgusting pads was the responsibility and duty of the user. An enameled bucket with a cover was purchased for my exclusive use. This was filled about half full of water to which laundry soap and Lysol had been added. The bucket was placed at the back of my clothes closet in readiness for the big event. As soon as a soiled pad was removed, it was immediately rinsed in cold water and put to soak in the pail of soap and Lysol until the monthly ordeal was over.

The first Monday morning after my flow stopped, I was required to arise early and scrub each pad on the washboard. Next they were boiled in more suds. Finally they were rinsed a couple of times and wrung out. After that they went into a blueing water rinse, run through the wringer again, and hung out to dry. I was exhorted to make sure when I hung them, that they were well hidden behind other laundry hanging on the line, lest someone walking past our home should see them. Immediately after school I was expected to rush home to take them in before any of the neighbors saw them. Once off the line they were ironed and taken up to my bedroom where I carefully folded, packaged, and again secreted them away in the bottom drawer of my bureau where they stayed until they were needed again.

With the advent of menstruation, a girl was expected to put away childish ways and to start acting in the manner of a little woman. By childish ways I mean such fun as hand springs, cartwheels, squat tag, roller skating, prisoner base, kick-the-can, capture-the-flag, jump rope, or any other rough and tumble activities in which children usually engage. The big fear the older women drummed into our heads was that any such conduct might cause our panties to be seen during the activity.

I had just turned fourteen when my turn came. From the moment of my first period, my old dresses were lengthened. All new clothes were tailored to reach down to my ankles. Regardless of my new status in the feminine world, I was still not allowed to wear high-heeled shoes. I could never convince my mother and grandmother that Mary Janes looked simply awful with long skirts.

Among the problems of yesteryear's family health were the incessant battles with everyday insects. Flies and mosquitoes were everywhere. The flies bred by the thousands in the livery stables and from the horse droppings in the street. Despite fly paper, fly swatters, screened windows, and screened doors, they still managed to get into the house. At least twice a day Mother flapped a dish towel to drive stubborn flies toward the door while one of us quickly opened the door to let them out.

While the mosquitoes multiplied in the gold dredger ponds located all around the town we were often vulnerable to their bites while we slept. Before we went to bed we were daubed with generous amounts of *Citronella*, supposedly to discourage the mosquitoes from biting. Despite precautions we often woke to find one or both eyes swollen shut. Nothing hurts worse than a mosquito bite on the ear which can itch for days.

My father was not a drinking man, but he did have one morning ritual which I assumed he did for health reasons. In his medicine cabinet he kept a bottle of whiskey or brandy and a shot glass. Each morning, after shaving and dressing, he poured an ounce of straight liquor and knocked it back in one gulp. I never saw him take more than one. I never asked him why he felt he needed the spirits. I assume he believed it was a tonic for his system.

My Grandma Westwood, being a midwife and practical nurse, had a locked room out on the farm where she kept her supply of "simples," Niter Water for fever, and the makings for mustard plasters. For colds, sore throats, and coughs, she had hore-hound and mullein syrups brewed from special leaves and brown sugar. She steeped these mixtures for hours on the back of the stove until they were thick as syrup. Most of the ointments and salves Grandma compounded were made from herbs with a tallow base. This, of course is where the word "simple" comes from. It means medicine made from herbs. She also had a quantity of sulfur and molasses for tonics to be used in the spring. Many of the bottles in her stock of medicines contained foul-smelling liniments.

In addition to all of these preparations she had a generous supply of bottles containing pills. Some were marked with a skull and crossbones. No child was allowed to step into *Simple Room* unless Grandma was with them. I was fascinated with the mysteries contained in that room. Because of my genuine interest, Grandma spent a great deal of time explaining all of their uses to me.

I loved the taste of her cough syrups, especially mullein and onion elixirs. I couldn't abide Grandma's concoction of sulfur and molasses. Despite our dislike and protestations, the sticky concoction was administered by the tablespoon every spring. Her bitter pills were dreadful even though her usual practice was to lodge them in a teaspoon of jelly or jam. The jelly slid down my throat easily and left the bitter pill stuck on my tongue.

With Grandma Westwood in the family we seldom needed a doctor. She came immediately if one of us should fall ill and stayed until we were well again. I can still see her in her white, freshly starched apron, bustling around the sick room in her joyful yet intensely efficient manner. While she was with us, she fed the patient rich chicken soup and eggnogs. The eggnog was laced with a dollop of whiskey or brandy for flavor.

To be one of Grandma's patients was a delightful experience. When I was ill, she sat for hours on the edge of my bed and entertained me with marvelous stories about life in England. With her in charge I felt safe, loved, and of course, well cared for.

10

Entertainment

My grandchildren and great-grandchildren have often asked me what we did for entertainment in our day without TV, radio, or tape recorders. The things one doesn't know about one doesn't miss.

Nearly every home owned a piano or pump organ, and children learned to play a musical instrument and had to practice for one hour each and every day whether they had talent or not.

We knew we had arrived musically when we could beat out *My Bonnie Lies Over the Ocean, A Bicycle Built for Two,* or *When You and I Were Young, Maggie.* That last tune was a particular favorite in our home, especially with my father because of the obvious connection with my mother's name.

When one was considered good enough, often to the performer's mortification, the entire family gathered around the piano for a sing-along. One was often paraded before company and called upon to entertain visitors. When I use the word "entertain," I use it very loosely.

At the farm Grandma Westwood played the pump organ and we belted out her favorite hymns. *Bringing in the Sheaves, Onward Christian Soldiers,* and *Amazing Grace* were real barnburners.

Because our family was Episcopalian we were allowed to play cards. If there were only our people, Whist or Pedro was the game of choice. If the group exceeded four, we gathered around the dining room table and played games like Pit, Old Maid, Fish or Rummy. These games sometimes went on as late as ten o'clock at night at which time our hostess served cake and coffee. When the mother of our hostess provided us with refreshment, it was a not too subtle hint that it was time to put away the cards and that the evening of fun and laughter had come to an end. It was time to start the process of saying goodnight.

Both of my parents belonged to The Lodge. Lodges were secret. If one's parents happened to be officers and were "going through the chairs," they had to study their parts. If you discovered one of them mumbling and pacing around the parlor with a look of concentration on their face, you knew for certain it was lodge business and it was wise to make yourself as scarce as possible until they were finished.

Lodge nights were special. Mother was often on her lodge's refreshment committee. No matter how late she returned home, she arrived with a plate full of odds and ends of cake. She then awakened my brother and me to enjoy slices of cake and a glass of warm milk to wash it down.

The women used their spare time for tea parties and formal visits. No one had the slightest idea that sugar was bad for a person, so beautiful cakes made from special and secret recipes were served. Every woman had at least one distinctive cake recipe for which she was known. She was expected to bring it whenever she was invited to any type of large gathering at which dessert was being served.

The Ladies' Aid Society filled many hours. Every church in town had one. During these meetings someone usually read to the assembled women from a good book or a specially prepared paper. The ladies kept their hands busy quilting, doing needlepoint, embroidering, sewing, or knitting. Often they prepared a layette for an expectant mother. This consisted of a set of clothes and bedding for the newborn.

One of the advantages of the extended family was the family picnic. These normally included at least three and sometimes four generations. We also had town, church, and neighborhood picnics to look forward to throughout the year.

The evening before Memorial Day, our family along with practically the entire town went out to the various cemeteries. We took our supper and ate sitting on the concrete curb which enclosed our family plot. On that evening the tombstones were scrubbed with scouring powder and brushes. Every weed was dug out and vases were filled with fresh cut flowers from our garden. Memorial Day gave us all a good feeling, knowing loved ones had been remembered.

The evening of work at the cemetery turned out to be quite a social affair. Much of the talk centered around friends and relatives who were dead and gone. The more recently they had died the more they were discussed. This was an admirable opportunity for the younger generation to learn some family history. We learned who was who, what they had done, and how they fit into the network we call the family. We were told in hushed voices who were the black sheep of the clan. Their graves were pointed out with a whispered warning not to follow in their footsteps.

After our family plot had been cleaned and decorated, the men took hoes and rakes and moved to Potter's Field for a clean-up job. While the men worked, the women prepared little bouquets of flowers for the unnamed graves.

Each church had an annual ice cream social held on the lawn of the Courthouse Square. There were some mouth-watering, strawberry festivals when that fruit was in season. I can still taste the strawberries and shortcake topped with whipped cream.

When strawberries were out of season, we paid fifteen cents for a huge dish of homemade ice cream and a generous slice of cake. You were allowed to pick any slice you wanted from a tray of cake. The affluent came back for seconds and thirds. These socials were the biggest money-making events for each of the churches.

These affable gatherings were big events that took days of work for everyone in the sponsoring committee. Every chair in each member's home was loaned to the church during the time of the soiree. Singers sang, musicians performed, and poetry was declaimed while children chased one another on the freshly mown lawn. When the day ended, it was more than evident that everyone had had a delightful time.

The Episcopalians and Catholics scandalized the Methodists and Congregationalists by roping off a part of the only paved street in town. The macadam was greased with shaved altar candles for a street dance. A small orchestra was hired, and we danced at ten cents a dance and drank iced lemonade at a nickel a glass.

The Fourth of July was usually one of the hottest days of the summer. Regardless of the heat, the entire town turned out to celebrate the grandest, non-religious observance of the year.

The celebration began with a procession of decorated bicycles, buggies, wagons, people on horseback, and a number of marching units. One group of marchers was the town band, replete in their dress uniforms. My father, all six-feet-two inches of him, marched proudly with the band as he played the trombone. After he lost his teeth, he kept time on the bass drum.

Next came the Grand Army of the Republic, decked out in frock coats with medals pinned onto their left breast. They wore navy blue Stetsons with a distinctive polished brass G.A.R. wreath gleaming on the crown. They were Union veterans of the War Between the States. There were no Confederate veterans. Thirty-five or forty years after the end of the rebellion, feelings were still running pretty high about that war. Californians were mighty proud their state was admitted as a Free State and supported the North. Even after the turn of the century there was still lingering bitterness against the South. The G.A.R. contingent was followed by a much younger group of veterans from the Spanish-American War. Oroville's militia made up another marching unit and furnished the color guard at the head of the parade.

A portion of the Oroville town band, circa 1900. *(Courtesy Butte County Historical Society)*

In a prominent place in the column were the volunteer firemen in their red shirts, wide leather belts, and leather helmets. They were splendid as they pulled their magnificent red and gold fire engine, followed by the hose wagons.

Oroville Fire Hall decorated for the Fourth of July. Note hand-pulled hose carts, circa 1900. *(Courtesy Butte County Historical Society)*

Members of the lodges marched in groups. The Masons participated, resplendent in frock coats with their white leather aprons tied around their waists. The Order of Redmen paraded, dressed as Indians, complete with feathers and war paint. The Oddfellows had a very showy drill team. There were many other lodges and fraternal contingents which included the Woodsmen of the World and the Eagles.

For this celebration the sidewalks were crowded with wives and the men who were not members of any of the groups on parade. We children, sitting with our feet in the gutter, clutched a balloon in one hand and an ice cream cone or a bag of freshly roasted peanuts in the other. We were enthralled with the spectacle passing before our eyes.

Our peanuts were purchased from an old Chinese man who answered to the descriptive name of Peanut Billy. He had two baskets full of peanuts in the shell, one on each end of a pole carried across his shoulders. In the bottom of each basket was a brazier of hot coals to keep the peanuts warm.

After everyone had passed in review, we went to the Courthouse Square. The veterans of the Civil War and the Spanish-American War, provided they were in uniform, were given the place of honor on the porch of the Courthouse. They were joined by the local ministers and priests and the speaker of the day. The flag was raised to the sound of a trumpet; then someone sang a patriotic song such as the *Star Spangled Banner* or *America the Beautiful.* A member of the clergy intoned a prayer, and someone solemnly declaimed Lincoln's Gettysburg Address or the Preamble to the Constitution. The speaker of the day talked long and, to us youngsters, boringly. Finally the band played a concert consisting of a few toe-tapping marches and patriotic music from previous wars. Then, as suddenly as it had started, the celebration was over.

When the festivities ended, we dragged ourselves home, thoroughly exhausted from the heat and excitement of the day. After supper my brother and our male cousins shot off their supply of firecrackers saved from the Chinese New Year's celebration the previous February. At the end of the day the grown-ups went to the community's annual Fourth of July dance.

The other big events of the year were the town dances. The Catholics put theirs on the weekend closest to March 17th, Saint Patrick's Day. The Oddfellows held theirs on the Fourth of July. The Firemen's Ball was held on New Year's Eve.

Father was a member of the volunteer fire department. In fact, every able-bodied Caucasian man who could afford a red flannel shirt, a belt, and a helmet could become a member provided he didn't get blackballed by the membership.

Fighting fires was serious business and imbued with a high level of community cooperation. When the fire bell rang, the volunteer firemen stopped whatever they were doing, slipped into their uniforms, and ran to Fireman's Hall. Their first task was to pull the fire engine and hose carts to the fire. After they had hooked their hoses to a fire hydrant, they pitched in and put their backs to the task of pumping water to fight the fire.

We had some terrible fires. Once the entire center of the town burned, including the livery stable and several horses. It was in the middle of the night and people came to the fire in nightgowns and robes. Women had cold cream on their faces and rag curlers in their hair. Men tucked their nightshirts into their trousers. They used everything they could lay their hands on to fight that fire. There were garden hoses, bucket brigades, and of course, fire hoses from the fire engine. As was customary, the building on fire usually burned to ashes. The firemen felt they had done a good job if they managed to keep the fire from spreading to adjoining buildings.

Strangely, fires turned into a sort of bizarre town entertainment as everyone turned out to watch the firemen do their duty and to cheer their victory when the fire was at last put out. If it looked like it was going to be a long fire, the women put together coffee and sandwiches to keep the men going. There was a good deal of back slapping and handshaking when the fire was extinguished and the exhausted firemen rolled up their hoses, packed up their gear and returned the pumper to the firehouse.

Oroville's band members went to band practice one evening a week. They were in constant demand for parades, dances, and Sunday evening concerts at the Courthouse Square. They were especially called upon for funerals. If anyone of consequence in the town died, the band marched before the hearse all the way to the cemetery. They played funeral dirges on the way out and when the funeral was over, marched home playing *It's a Hot time in the Old Town Tonight* or some other tune just as raucous.

Summers were hot and, thank goodness, the cooling waters of the Feather River were handy. All of us learned to swim at an early age, usually without the knowledge or consent of our parents. We learned in the dredger ponds by holding onto an empty, plugged up, coal oil can.

The Feather River was swift, wide, and unforgiving. You either became a good swimmer or you drowned. Our parents sat on the bank in agony while we shot the rapids or swam across the river and back.

The suit I wore while I learned to swim consisted of a panty waist made of muslin. This was an undergarment worn by little girls which consisted of two pieces with short pants buttoning to the shirt at the waist. When I was old enough to start swimming in the river, Grandmother made me a swim suit with serge bloomers and puffed sleeves. Of course, the suit had to have a skirt. I wore a bandanna around my head and long black stockings on my legs and rubber swim shoes to protect my feet. It was a beautiful suit to look at, but I found swimming much easier when I wore only the panty waist.

The boys used the dredger ponds for still another use. They built rafts out of scrap wood and small logs and pretended they were shipwrecked or pirates. My brother and our cousin Earl went out on one dredger pond on a raft they had built. The pond they had chosen to play in was full of a sort of slimy quicksand. Bill fell in and immediately started to sink up to his arm pits in the muck. Earl managed to find a plank and crawled out to pull him out. By the time they were finished the two boys were covered with mud. They came home, sneaked into the house and took a bath. When Mother and Grandmother discovered what was happening they weren't very happy, especially when they saw what a wreck Bill and Earl had made of their freshly cleaned bathroom.

When we were in the seventh grade we started having "surprise" birthday parties. They were customarily held on Saturday afternoon. The guest of honor ordinarily helped plan his or her own party. The invited met at the Courthouse. After that, we paired off and walked to the party with our best beau. Kissing games such as Spin-the-Bottle were the backbone of these parties. The games were accompanied with giggling, blushing, squealing, and teasing.

By the time I graduated from grammar school I had learned to dance. A man and his wife came to town and opened a dance studio. They offered a six-week course in ballroom dancing which consisted of two lessons a week. This cost folks the staggering sum of ten dollars. The classes were made up of eighth and ninth graders plus a few high school students. We met at four in the afternoon on Wednesdays and Fridays.

The ten-dollar tuition included punch and cookies which were served halfway through each lesson. The entire concept of the course was to teach us ballroom manners and a few of the more common dance steps. The boys had to wear white gloves. This was mandatory in ballroom etiquette to prevent their sweaty hands from staining our frocks. We learned the Butterfly Waltz, Fox Trot, Tango, Paul Jones, and of course, the Virginia Reel. Once we had learned the intricacies of ballroom dancing and deportment, we had high school dances once a month on Saturday night.

Our high school did not have an auditorium, but the Episcopal Guild Hall, only a block away, was used for school functions. The dances were well chaperoned by our parents and the Episcopal priest and his wife. At 11:45 the priest announced that the last dance was about to begin. After that, we waltzed until midnight to the tune of *Good Night Ladies*.

We had all arrived at the stage of beau and girlfriend. We even went so far as to hold hands and give our beaus a very chaste good night kiss. All of these things we kept secret, even from our best friends. Ballroom dancing classes were one of the most beautiful and wonderful experiences of my young life.

Oroville had another dance hall open to the public and only attended by purportedly disreputable people known as "riffraff." Our parents wouldn't have allowed us to go there, but I must admit we were all curious about what went on inside that place.

The men in our family often used whatever spare time they had to go hunting or fishing. Uncle John's farm had a large pond and was an excellent place to shoot ducks, quail, pheasants, and rabbits which became a part of our diet.

With all of the activities we had—swimming, hiking to Table Mountain, basketball, tennis, the Music Club, Literary Club, our amateur theatrical performances, and our numerous parties and dances—we kept pretty busy.

11

Personal Comments

My brother Bill had beautiful blue eyes, blond curly hair, perfect features, and a small mouth. He was also tall and handsome and my mother adored him. In addition he was an excellent student and was consistently at the top of his class. He was a very talented and accomplished piano player who was able to perform from memory beautiful sonatas and other complicated selections.

When we played games, he invariably took charge and was the boss. When we quarreled, I was usually the one who was in the wrong at least in my mother's eyes, and would get the spanking and then be sent to my room.

I, on the other hand, had a large mouth and straight red hair. To make matters worse, my face was covered with large round freckles. As if that wasn't enough, I was skinny as a fence post. The green-eyed monster took over when I was quite young. For a time I was sure I had been adopted. When Grandma Westwood explained to me that she thought I was a beautiful baby when she delivered me, I was sure she had made it up and only said so out of kindness. One of my proofs for thinking I was adopted was that Mother had black hair and blue eyes and father was quite blond. Where my red hair came from was hard to explain. The only mitigating factor in favor of my legitimate parentage was the fact that father had a red moustache.

Phoebe Louise Westwood
(1896-1984), circa 1908.
(Rohrbacher Family Collection)

My entire outlook on life changed when I was eight. I attended my first legitimate theatre production, a matinee of *Little Lord Fauntleroy* at the Oroville theatre. In those days, legitimate theatre road companies came to Oroville three or four times a year and played for six nights plus a Saturday matinee. From that day on theatre became my world. I wrote plays, then directed them. It seemed only logical that since I authored and directed the play I should cast myself in the lead. The fun of writing plays was that I crafted the female lead to fit my own personality and looks.

Heady with all of this theatrical success, I found it relatively easy to talk my parents into financing elocution lessons. I studied hard and learned the actor's skills of rendition, enunciation, eloquence, pronunciation, articulation, delivery and diction.

Hello Central, Give Me Heaven was my favorite of all the pieces I memorized. This selection was about a little girl whose mother was dead and much missed by her. Another favorite was *The Little Match Girl*. This one described a poor little girl who sold matches and artificial flowers and eventually froze to death in the snow. It had a happy ending as she went directly to heaven. How I must have bored my family and friends with my recitations!

I never got over the "theatre bug." In grammar school, high school, and at the University of California, I auditioned for every play that was produced. I didn't always get the lead, but seldom was I not cast. After I gained some experience, I did get more than my share of leads.

During the time I was a student at Berkeley I spent every spare penny I could for theatre tickets. I went to the Fulton Theatre to see stars like Lunt and Fontanne or Minnie Maddern Fiske. Sometimes I took the ferry across the bay to Percy William's Orpheum in San Francisco to see headliners like Billy Burke, Al Jolson, Burns and Allen, and countless others who later became film, radio, and then, much later, television personalities. The Orpheum circuit had the best of all the talent available.

As time passed and my brother and I matured, I came to love him dearly in spite of the fact he often made fun of how thin I was. Once he remarked that my legs were so skinny and my feet were so big "they looked like two toothpicks stuck into a couple of smoked oysters." Despite remarks like that, as we headed toward our college years, I found it was good to have a beautiful big brother. It was especially good when he squired me to dances and told me he would rather dance with me than any other girl in the room.

My brother did get himself into trouble now and then. One time he and our cousin Lloyd stole a couple of cigars from our father's supply. They went out behind the wood shed to smoke them. When Dad came home, he noticed his supply of cigars had been tampered with. He knew right where to go to set things straight. He didn't rant and rave. All he did was call the boys in and say in a nice voice, "You know, I think it's about time you boys learned to smoke." With that he took two cigars, clipped the ends and handed one to each of the boys. "I'll light them for you," he said as he held out a lit match. He watched them as they smoked and smoked the cigars. It wasn't long until they turned green. When he felt they were sick enough, he took the cigars and said, "Now boys, don't ever bother my cigars in the future." I don't think they ever did.

As I entered my teen years people began to say nice things about my thick auburn hair, and boys in our crowd seemed to like me. I even dared to believe my destiny in life was not to be an old maid but one day to marry.

Every young woman was expected to keep a clean and tidy home and place three square meals on the table each day. The bridegroom was obligated by custom to provide a home and the means for support.

The young bride brought into marriage as a part of her dowry, pots and pans, at least one set of dishes, sheets, pillowcases, towels, and enough dish towels to set-up housekeeping. As part of her trousseau she was expected to bring with her enough personal clothing to take care of her needs for at least the first year of their marriage.

Most engagements lasted a year or longer. This gave the girl's family enough time to make all necessary preparations to launch her in a satisfactory manner. It was a matter of pride to the mother of the bride that her daughter was prepared with the proper skills for her new life's responsibilities. It was very important to her that her daughter could fix wholesome meals, sew from a pattern, do mending and alterations, knit and darn socks, maintain an ordered house, and be generally competent to take on all of the responsibilities of a homemaker. To this end, I, along with my friends, had a hope chest. Each birthday and Christmas, family, friends, and relatives contributed to our bridal gifts. From the moment we entered our teens we collected recipes and practiced cooking for the family with mother as mentor and supervisor.

Our hope chests contained a good supply of kitchen and fancy aprons. Any woman who cared about her appearance never thought of venturing into the kitchen without an apron to protect her dress. Once the preparations for supper were completed she changed from her kitchen apron into a more attractive tea apron. I can't recall ever seeing my mother or grandmother without a fancy apron on during a meal. This way they were protected if they went out to the kitchen to replenish something for the meal or to bring on the dessert.

While I was growing up, I had a best girlfriend, Mona. When we were about thirteen, a girl named Cora took it upon herself to teach our group the facts of life. What she taught us was not about butterflies and the birds and bees, but the real facts. Cora pointed out two pregnant women in our neighborhood and then proceeded to tell us in minute detail how they got that way. We were shocked and avoided Cora from that day onward.

Both Mona and I felt pretty dirty about the whole thing. As much as we didn't want to believe Cora, we knew deep down she was probably onto something that girls our age had no business knowing. The thing that made us angry was our feeling we had lost some of our innocence. We wondered, in our youthful naiveté, how our parents could possibly have performed such a disgusting act.

Our familiarity with Mona's two brothers and my one plus our numerous boy cousins did tend to substantiate Cora's message about the male anatomy and how babies were conceived. Eventually we had to accept the truth for what it was. After the first shock of learning the "awful truth," Mona and I found that "dirty talk" was not all that interesting and steered away from further intimate discussions.

At the turn of the century, if a girl was foolish enough to get herself into trouble, it became a real tragedy for all concerned. Once the word spread around, and it did, both the girl's family and the boy's family were in terrible disgrace all over town. They became the objects of pity and scorn. In most cases the young couple were forced to get married. If they stayed in the area, they were looked down upon for the rest of their lives. They were known as the couple who "had to get married." People were endowed with long memories and were not very forgiving.

When a girl married, there was an unofficial count in people's minds to see if a baby was born to the couple in less than the conventional nine months. If a child was born in less than the normal time, there was usually an announcement that it was premature. This often worked provided the baby was small and presented itself only a few weeks early. In my day, getting pregnant out of wedlock was one thing you could never live down.

For my part, and I'm sure it was the same for most of my friends, I never dared be anything but a "good girl." Until the day I was married, petting could go no further than kissing and hugging. If a boy became too aggressive he was promptly told off and given his "walking papers." Our group were all good girls and none of us kept steady company with a boy. Our parents frowned on the idea of young people pairing off. We sort of shared our boyfriends and waited to see which boy would ask which girl to the next party.

At the dances our entire gang sat together and the girls' dance cards were quickly filled. The boys we liked best were allowed two nonconsecutive dances. Our escort usually had the first and last dance and one in the middle.

Around our junior year in high school, some of the boys ducked outside between numbers and came back smelling of tobacco. Occasionally they had liquor on their breath. If we smelled alcohol, we would immediately ask to sit down. Boys who had been drinking tended to become a bit too aggressive while dancing. The chaperones kept their eyes open for anything untoward on the dance floor. If they caught a couple dancing too close, the offenders were immediately pulled aside and given a good dressing down. If an escort of any girl failed to behave, he was unacceptable to our crowd for future dates. He became *persona non grata*. To some of our classmates we were known as the Snobby Six. A better name might have been the Silly Six.

We were a close-knit group. What with slumber parties, bicycle trips, skating parties, hikes, and our impromptu get-togethers around the piano, we were pretty busy and had very little time to get ourselves into real trouble.

The word "gay" had an entirely different meaning then than it does today. Gay meant being happy or, when it was applied to a person, it described one with a blithe spirit. I had never heard the term homosexual. If I had, I wouldn't have known what in the world it meant. To my knowledge, we had only two "unusual" people in Oroville.

One was Sadie, who was quite a gal. She was an enormous woman, close to six feet tall. She kept her hair cut short like a man's and wore men's shoes, shirts, and jackets, and an ankle-length black skirt.

Sadie lived in a cabin in the hills where she earned her living by cutting and splitting oak for firewood which she sold to town people by the cord.

The day she made deliveries, she unloaded her wood, stacked it neatly in the woodshed, collected her money, and then drove off in her wagon. When she arrived she never spoke except to say, "I brought your firewood." When she finished unloading her wagon and stacking the firewood, she asked, "I'm done. Do you pay or shall I collect from the mister?" The only time we saw her was a couple of times a year when she made wood deliveries.

The other individual in our town was different. He was referred to by everyone in town as Lord Tavener. To find a more gentlemanly human being, one would have to look hard and long. He was from England and was known as a remittance man. This is a nice way of saying his family paid him to stay away from home. He kept a permanent room at the Union Hotel. I never discovered why he chose Oroville as his American home. Once a month he went to the bank to deposit his remittance from England.

When he first arrived in Oroville, he spent his time at the library reading. Other times he took long walks in the hills. While hunting he dressed in plus fours, which are baggy, below the knees knickers over heavy woolen socks. He also wore a hunting jacket and carried a shotgun. To my knowledge, he never killed any game.

Eventually he became an important member of the town and gained the respect of virtually all of the residents of Oroville. He was an active member of the Episcopal Church and worked as an unpaid assistant to the priest. He played the organ, directed the choir, kept the parish books, planned activities for young people, and visited the sick. He was well loved by everyone who knew him.

Lord Tavener returned to England when he was a very old man. I never heard why he left California to return to his family. I imagine the older people in his family, the ones who had sent him away, had passed on and there was no longer any reason for him to stay in the United States. He was very much missed by his many Oroville friends.

I didn't have the slightest idea of what Lord Tavener's problem was until I was sixteen. At that time I read a book called *Wells of Loneliness*. After reading that book my eyes were opened, and I had some understanding of Lord Tavener and Sadie's problem. It was only then that I began to understand and appreciate what personal pain he must have suffered at the hands of his family. I also gained some awareness of how this beautiful and talented man had adjusted to his being different from the majority of people around him. I sincerely hope he was received by his English relatives with open arms and was as loved by them as he was by his California friends.

12

Clothes and Shopping

Everything our family wore was made at home except suits for my father and shirt collars, which were either done by a tailor or were procured ready made. Only wealthy families had all of their clothing made by a tailor or seamstress. Women's hats came from the town milliner.

Shopping in the dry goods stores was mostly for yardage and trimmings. Most families had a sewing lady who came in at least once a year and stayed for a week making outfits for the family. Not us; we had Grandmother!

Grandmother made all of my father and brother's shirts, night clothes, and BVDs except winter long johns.

Girls were taught at an early age to sew by hand, hemstitch, embroider, knit, and crochet. Once they learned enough to pass muster with the women in the family, they were expected to do their share.

Grandmother's Singer sewing machine and chest full of materials were constantly in use. We called the contents of the chest "findings." In this huge box she kept bolts of material to make nightgowns. Out of a bolt came night shirts for my father and brother. Tennis flannel for men came in varieties of striped patterns or plaids. Women's flannel patterns were of little flowers. Hardly a day passed, except Sunday and Monday, without her doing some sewing or mending.

To keep a man's cuffs from showing wear they were ripped off and turned. Most collars were detachable and were turned when they became threadbare.

Everything we used of cloth was made at home. Sheets, pillow slips, shams, splashers (to go behind the washstands), and dishtowels had to be hemmed and trimmed. Table napkins and handkerchiefs were rolled and hemmed by hand. These were mostly stitched when the women went to tea parties. Men's nightshirts and work shirts were homemade as were women's aprons, petticoats, panties, shimmies, and corset covers. The women's articles were ruffled and trimmed with lace or embroidery.

Grandmother made my dresses roomy with large hems so they could be let out as I grew. There was a wire frame dress form on which both Mother and Grandmother's dresses were draped while they were being constructed. This meant they didn't have to stand around waiting for fittings. I wasn't quite that lucky. My fate was to stand on a stool for what seemed like hours. I got a wallop on the bottom if I jiggled or wiggled too much. I was also stuck with pins quite often. Fittings were an ordeal one had to endure.

No respectable woman thought of going out of the house with less than two half petticoats under her dress. The inner petticoat usually had one ruffle. The outside petticoat had three or more ruffles designed to hold her skirts out. They wore a camisole on top. It came straight across the front with straps over the shoulders. In the straps and across the front was beading; the ribbons had to be run through all the little loops and tied with a bow in the front. In addition to the camisole and petticoats women wore panties with wide legs. They were split in the crotch so when a lady went to the toilet the slit was opened and there was no need to take them down.

During the summer, for underclothes I wore an undershirt and a knitted panty waist called a Ferris vest. All around the bottom of the vest were buttons. Around the top of my panties and my two half petticoats were button holes which matched the placement of the buttons on the vest. This was so everything could be fastened securely to the Ferris vest. On my legs I wore long black stockings on weekdays. On Sunday they were replaced with white stockings. The stockings were fastened to garters attached to a garter belt snugly secured around my waist.

Over the petticoat on weekdays I wore a multicolored gingham dress. The cotton patterns my grandmother picked out for me were usually in brightly colored stripes, checks, and plaids. On Sundays I was decked out in batiste, a white, fine, thin cloth made of cotton or wool.

During the really hot months the white dress was usually made of organdy, a thin, stiff, nearly transparent material which was used both for dresses and sheer curtains. Over all of this went a sleeveless dress called a pinafore. During the winter we sported long sleeved and legged woolen underwear. Over that we wore a shirtwaist and two flannel petticoats, This was topped off with a dress made of wool. Then came the old familiar pinafore. A typical pinafore would have been made of blue checked gingham trimmed with embroidery for every day and white organdy trimmed in lace for church on Sunday or on Saturday evenings when we went downtown.

Neither child nor adult of either sex thought of leaving the house without a hat on their head. Boys sported caps of some description. The fedora was the hat of choice for most men. This is a soft felt hat with a curved brim with the crown creased lengthwise from front to back. Some men wore derbies or bowlers which were by far the favorite hat of traveling salesmen, called drummers.

Twice a year most women and girls purchased a new hat. A trip to Mrs. Woolever's millinery shop on Bird Street was a very special occasion. The sign, in bold gold letters on her window, read:

MRS. S. WOOLEVER
IMPORTER AND DESIGNER OF FINE MILLINERY

During our twice-yearly visit to the milliner, each of us usually took an old felt hat to be cleaned, blocked, and re-trimmed. Springtime was the opportunity to look over the latest poke bonnets and to pick the trimmings for a new Easter bonnet. In September, Mrs. Woolever's shop was stocked with the latest winter shapes and styles.

When we reached the age of about nine, we no longer wore poke bonnets. We had graduated to leghorn hats. The leghorn had a wide, round brim and a shallow crown and was made of very fine, plaited, yellow straw. There wasn't much to decide about when it came to trimming one of these hats. They had a black velvet ribbon around the crown which was tied in the back. Long streamers hung down to the middle of the wearer's back. English school girls still wear them as part of their uniform in some of their private schools.

Mother and Grandmother wore hats gorgeous with exotic trimmings. There were many choices of color, material, texture, and trim. For example, there were velvet roses and silk flowers, pom-poms, or flowing scarves of chiffon to adorn their summer straws. In the winter they turned to feather willow plumes, ostrich feathers or stuffed birds perched atop their felt and velvet bonnets.

Because of their black hair, Mother and Grandmother always had some shade of red trim on their hats. I couldn't wear red as it clashed with my auburn hair.

When I was ten, my father called me aside and told me, "I would like to give your mother a hat for her birthday. You go down to Mrs. Woolever and plan the hat." After discussing it for a few minutes, I asked him how much he wanted to spend. He indicated seven dollars was about right. The going rate for an ordinary woman's hat was five dollars. The one I picked out was a black velvet. It was a variation of a poke bonnet, which is a bonnet with a projecting brim. To set off my mother's jet black hair I chose to have the underside lined with red. The hat also had a colorful plume which came swooping back on one side and a red velvet rose attached to the front. This turned out to be Mother's most elegant hat. It set off her deep blue eyes and made her wavy black hair look like polished cobalt. Styles didn't change very often so she wore that lovely hat for at least ten years.

The Sears Roebuck catalog was a great source of ideas for the latest styles being worn in the East. We called this catalog "The Wish Book." Dad didn't like us to order things from Sears unless they couldn't be purchased in Oroville. He felt it was better to keep our trade in town.

On Sunday girls wore black, patent leather Mary Janes. These really stood out against our long white stockings. Before the shoes were put away, I had to grease them with Vaseline before carefully wrapping them in tissue paper and placing them back in their shoe box until the next Sunday. During the rest of the week we all wore black, low heeled, high top, buttoned shoes. Much to Bill's and my distress, Mother bought our shoes one size larger so we wouldn't outgrow them before they had been resoled at least once.

I didn't pay much attention to what the adults wore on their feet. I do know that every lady had a button hook on her bureau. That means they probably wore high button shoes at least part of the time. There must have been some kind of low cut shoe for the ladies because Mother and Grandmother occasionally wore gaiters, a covering for the lower leg or ankle made of felt or soft leather. They had buttons on the outside and a strap under the instep and were considered quite dressy. My father wore black or brown high top shoes.

Women wore a great deal more clothing than they do today. It took a prodigious amount of sewing to keep a family properly dressed.

Father had his three-piece suits and overcoats made by the tailor. The vests had real pockets in which he carried a gold watch and chain with his lodge medallion hanging from it. Men and boys wore suspenders instead of belts to hold their pants up.

My brother's shirts were different from Dad's. Boys usually wore knee pants with over the calf stockings. Dad's old trousers were cut down by Grandmother into short pants or knickers for my brother. His pants were made much too large for him and pulled up with suspenders. The shirt wasn't tucked in but went on over the suspenders. At the bottom of the shirt was a draw string which was pulled tight at the waist. As he grew, the suspenders were let out, which lowered the trousers. This style of dress tended to give the boys a sort of baggy look.

Men who worked in offices or clerked in stores took off their coats and hung them, along with their hats, on a clothes rack. Then they slipped on black sleeve protectors which covered their cuffs and the sleeves of their shirts to a little above their elbows. The sleeve protectors had elastic at both ends to keep them in place. Clerks in stores usually also wore aprons to cover their vests.

I was required to trim the women's undergarments and roll and hem handkerchiefs and table linen. I learned to knit and crochet well enough to knit socks for my father and brother.

During the summer months we started preparing homemade Christmas gifts. This included knitting socks for the men, making and hemstitching handkerchiefs with fancy embroidered initials, or crocheting something for Mother or Grandmother. I found, at that time of the year, if I went into my bedroom with my sewing basket and closed the door, no one dared to disturb me. Everyone took it for granted I was making something for a Christmas surprise. This gave me the opportunity to read forbidden books without running the risk of being caught. I hid these books under my mattress. Eventually I became quite adept at knitting or crocheting and reading at the same time. Our so-called prohibited books were mighty tame by today's standards.

13

Transportation

L adies walked, men rode bicycles or horses, and
children hopped, skipped, and ran to go downtown.
My family did not own a horse and buggy for the
simple reason there was really no reason to. Every place
in town was within walking distance. Everything we
needed to buy was delivered to our door. When we went
to Grandma's farm for Christmas or other holidays or
wanted to go on a family outing, Father hired a surrey
from the livery stable.

If we wanted to go on a big outing with friends,
relatives, and neighbors, everyone chipped in to hire the
tallyho. The tallyho, which came complete with a
teamster to drive it, was an omnibus. It was a double
decker rig pulled by four, matched horses and seated
twenty-four people. It had ample room for picnic
hampers, blankets, and pillows.

Our usual outings were to a place north of Oroville called Table Mountain. This was one of the most beautiful places in the vicinity. It was also a very popular spot for a picnic because in the spring there was a beautiful waterfall, a grassy picnic area, and trees to provide plenty of shade.

If we wanted to go to the mountains to visit my mother's sisters who lived at Paradise and Magalia, we traveled by stagecoach. I once asked how Paradise got its name. I was told that it was originally called Pair o' Dice and over the years the words were contracted into the name of Paradise. At any rate, it was a twenty-five mile trip. On an excursion of this length, we stopped at Twelve Mile House for dinner and a change of horses.

About 1906 the Northern Electric started operating between Oroville and Chico. Later service was extended between Oroville and Marysville and eventually all the way down to Sacramento. The Northern Electric line was nicknamed the *En Nee*. Compared to the Western Pacific, the ride on the *En Nee* was a rough and jolting one. Everyone used to joke that one tended to travel as far sideways as forward as the cars jostled and jolted over the rough roadbed.

In 1910, with the completion of the Feather River project and the building of a bridge across the upper bay, the Western Pacific completed the line between Oakland and Salt Lake City. The first through train from Oakland stopped in Oroville filled with dozens of newspaper reporters and dignitaries. It must have taken that first train days and days to finally make it to Salt Lake City because it stopped at nearly every town it came through for speeches and a rousing celebration.

The Livery Stable Corral at Bird and Downer Streets, owned by T. C. Lee, circa 1900. (Courtesy Butte County Historical Society)

The Oroville and Quincy State Company passenger and mail coach, circa 1900. *(Courtesy Butte County Historical Society)*

This was a big occasion for Oroville. The entire town turned out to see the train and to join in the festivities. The train was met by the mayor, city fathers, and, of course, the town band. After a few speeches, much picture taking, flag waving, and all other essential pageantry deemed necessary for such an occasion, the conductor cried "All aboard!" and the train, to the strains of band music, much cheering and hand waving from the townspeople, slowly chugged away from the platform.

Our family's life of mobility changed when Father bought an automobile. It was a Willis Overland. The year was 1903. Our model was topless and entered by a step that lowered at the back. The center of the back seat lifted to make an entrance. Ours was a five-seater, two bucket seats in the front with a back seat big enough for three adults.

Because of the unpaved roads, the dust that billowed up and over the passengers was unbelievable. To protect our clothing, every member of the family had a linen duster and a matching cap. Mine had a blue velvet collar. My cap had a matching blue veil that went all the way around the top and tied in place. Ladies and girls had chiffon scarves which buttoned onto the cap with the ends tied at the back. When the dust was too bad, we untied the scarf and pulled it over our faces. The male members of the family always sat in the front and wore goggles. If it rained we stayed home.

The roads left much to be desired. They were unpaved and were bumpy, crooked, and contained plenty of sharp glass and nails which had fallen from wagons. Most nails had worked their way out of horses' hooves.

It was a successful trip indeed which didn't produce at least one puncture.

When one did get a puncture, there were no automobile clubs to call to send someone out to fix it. Every car carried a minimum of one spare tire, a jack, tire irons, wrenches, a patching kit, and a hand pump. Most men became expert roadside puncture fixers.

The automobile opened a whole new world of mobility to the members of our family. We visited places like Gridley (eighteen miles away), Chico, and Marysville. These towns were at least twenty-five miles from Oroville. Sundays, if we felt adventurous, we took a trip to visit Mother's relatives up in the mountains around Magalia and Paradise.

On the twelve-mile ride out to Grandma's farm, there was a dip in the road we used to call a "thank you ma'am." When we went over that dip, Bill and I thought the sensation of going down and then abruptly up again was nearly as exciting as the Big Dipper Roller Coaster at Santa Cruz. So, unless we were in a terrible hurry, Dad turned into the next farm and went back over the "thank you ma'am." Then he'd turn around and take us over it again.

The road to Grandma's farm was on the levee of the Feather River and curved around like a snake. The countryside was full of beautiful smells. When we traveled out of town, the air was full of the aroma of the orange groves, alfalfa fields, ripe fruit, olive trees in bloom, and the river. Believe it or not, even a field spread with fresh manure had a pleasant and distinctively earthy smell. Of all the wonderful fragrances in the whole wide world, none could surpass that of the sea breeze when we drove to the coast.

Later on, my parents had larger, better, faster automobiles, but none was as thrilling as our first car, our little Willis Overland.

The year we got our automobile was the same year the Wright brothers flew at Kittyhawk. Heavier than air flight caused a terrific sensation in the minds of everyone. The idea that those two men were brave enough to climb into a machine made of wood, cloth, and metal that needed an engine and propellers to get it off the ground and then to make the contraption fly seemed magical. There were pictures in the paper showing their plane and stories about how many minutes they stayed up in the air. Dad read aloud to the family the wonderful, exciting exploits of the Wright brothers.

It wasn't too many years before the first airplanes came to town. They were flown by daring young men who the older generation considered foolhardy daredevils. If any fool was brave enough he could pay a dollar and go up for a ride over the town. My friends and I thought pilots were dashing, devil-may-care types who lived exciting lives.

By 1914, when World War I had just started in Europe, pilot daredevils were beginning to do stunt flying. At the 1915 Pan Pacific Exposition I watched in horror while a famous pioneer flier named Beechie fell to his death while doing stunts.

14

Summer Heat

Summers in Oroville were long, hot, and dry so we took whatever steps we could to stay cool as possible. Immediately after breakfast, the shades in the bedrooms, parlor sitting room, and dining room were pulled down. At the same time every window in the house except in the kitchen were closed. In this way, the cool air from the night was kept in the house and the outside heat from the broiling sun was kept out. The door separating the kitchen from the rest of the house was closed tightly. The windows in the kitchen were left open as was the screened back door. The reason for this was because the wood stove had to go full blast all day regardless of the outside temperature. To keep the air in the house circulating we had a ceiling fan in the dining room and an electric fan in the sitting room.

The bedrooms on the west side of the house turned into bake ovens in the afternoon and remained that way long after the sun went down. Before bedtime we slipped into our bedrooms to open the windows and hoped for a cooling evening breeze to dissipate some of the heat that had collected during the heat of the day.

Later on we were one of the fortunate families who had a sleeping porch. This was built on top of the woodshed. It was one large room with screens all the way around. In order to have a semblance of privacy from neighbors' prying eyes, we had roll awnings made of split bamboo. Dad strung wires and Mother hung muslin curtains as partitions between the beds.

When it was time for bed, we retired to our bedrooms to undress and slip into our night clothes. Once in our robes and slippers we scurried down the back steps into the backyard and up the steps leading to the sleeping porch.

When everyone was in bed and the lights were turned out, Mother made sure we were decently covered. She then pulled up the awnings. In that way, if there was a cooling breeze of any kind, we received full benefit from it. Provided we didn't have mosquitoes buzzing around our ears, we got a comfortable night's sleep.

In the morning, we quickly pulled on our robes and slippers and dashed upstairs to wash and dress. It was quite an experience to have men and women sleeping in one room.

On those wonderful summer evenings, as we sat on the front lawn enjoying a pitcher of ice tea with neighbors, we often looked at the stars and the moon and wondered what the people, if any, who lived on them were like. We speculated if perhaps they were sitting on their lawns, looking down on our planet, and wondering about us.

Towns were much darker because there weren't neon signs, street lights, and all the other extraneous illumination we find in cities these days. This meant the stars twinkled and the moon shone clearly and brightly. Father knew the names of most of the constellations and pointed them out for us. Dad taught us to locate and recognize the North Star, the Big and Little Dippers, the Milky Way, the planets in our solar system, and most of the major constellations.

If it was an exceptionally hot evening, my brother and I were allowed to strip down to our underwear and run through the sprinkler before we went to bed.

Later on, Father rigged up a shower in the woodshed. The shower was made from a coal oil can with nail holes on the bottom. A garden hose was used to fill the can with water. The shower served two purposes. It not only got us clean, but it cooled us off. It took two people to take a shower—one person to turn the water on and off and the other to take the shower. A woman or girl could only wash one side at a time because she had to be careful to pull her waist length hair aside so as not to get it wet.

Because of malaria and to escape the heat of an Oroville summer, the entire family, except Father, went to the seashore at Santa Cruz for our summer vacation. We made the trip in the middle of June and stayed the rest of June, all of July, and the first two weeks of August.

Western Pacific's morning train came through Oroville at the ungodly hour of four o'clock. Its final destination was the Oakland Mole. Father got us to the station in plenty of time to catch that early morning train. As he kissed us all good-bye and told us to mind our mother, he added the promise that he would see us at the end of July.

The express wagon picked up our immense steamer trunk the day before we left. This one piece of baggage contained all the clothing and other essentials needed for our entire eight-week vacation. Mother had a very firm rule: "If it doesn't fit in the trunk, it doesn't go."

In addition to our picnic basket, Mother carried one piece of hand luggage onto the train. This bag was known as a telescope basket. A telescope basket, true to its name, has two parts that slide one inside the other like the tubes of a telescope. Luggage of this sort could be expanded or contracted as more items were added to or taken from the contents. This bag contained our night clothes, toilet articles, and one change of clothes for each of us. The picnic hamper was full of food, including sandwiches, fried chicken, potato salad, cookies, and cake to eat on the trip.

The train arrived at the Oakland Mole at about ten in the morning. Aunt Florence, who lived in San Francisco, met our train in Oakland to help Mother with my brother and me to board the ferry that took us across to the San Francisco Ferry Building.

Clam chowder on the ferry was delicious and we always had a bowl during the crossing. The specialty was Coney Island style made with tomato sauce and served in a deep, round, white bowl. The soup was full of clam meat and square-cut chunks of potato. With the generous serving of chowder they served a soup bowl full of oyster crackers.

I enjoyed standing on the upper deck of the ferry with a fresh breeze blowing in my face as we approached the skyline of San Francisco. On the right, at a distance, was Alcatraz Island and beyond was Angel Island. Much closer, also on the right, was Yerba Buena Island. On a clear day, one could see all the way to the Golden Gate and beyond to the blue Pacific Ocean. As we neared San Francisco, the clock on the Ferry Building, which dominated the skyline, loomed larger and larger with each passing minute.

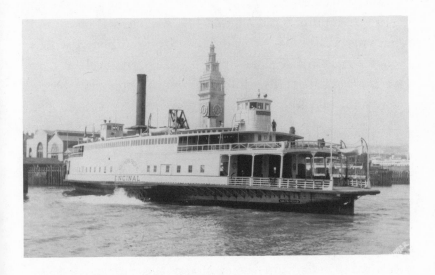

The ferry boat *Encinal* entering the ferry slip at San Francisco, circa 1910. *(Courtesy California State Library Collection)*

The thrill of heightened anticipation increased with the sensation that traveled up through our feet from the ferry as it vibrated and shook as it was thrown into reverse just before we docked. I loved the way it squeaked and squealed in protest as its bow slid into the slip and the wood sides of the ship made contact with the piling on each side of the pier. That glorious ride across the bay from the Oakland Mole to the Ferry Building was the best part of the trip to Santa Cruz.

Bill and I walked in wonder through the cavernous expanses of the ferry terminal. Each summer I was amazed at the numbers of people coming and going through the place. When we finally emerged onto the street, we took the horse-drawn street car up Market Street to Haight Street, which was only a block from Aunt Florence's home.

After dinner and a short rest we left for Third and Townsend in plenty of time to board Southern Pacific's train to Santa Cruz. The narrow gauge train left at four in the afternoon. Its route took us through Half Moon Bay and then followed the coast to our destination. The sweep of the Pacific Ocean viewed from the train was spectacular. When we were a little older and Mother felt she could trust us not to fall off, she allowed my brother and me to go to the back platform of the observation car and take in the marvelous panorama.

Our train arrived in Santa Cruz at about eight-thirty that evening. Although we were exhausted, we were thrilled by the cool breezes and the distinctive salty fragrance of the ocean. After we had collected our trunk from the station's baggage room, we clambered aboard the courtesy surrey sent by the St. George Hotel, where we spent one night. The next day Mother arranged for housekeeping rooms for our eight weeks' stay in Santa Cruz.

Our vacations at the coast were marvelous. All summer long we went to the beach daily, armed with a picnic hamper, beach towels and swimming suits.

The Santa Cruz Boardwalk and Pavilion, circa 1910.
(Courtesy California State Library Collection)

Suntans were not popular, so even while swimming, I had to wear a hat or sun bonnet. In spite of these precautions, the reflected sun off the water and white sand still caused my nose to burn and peel. Much to my disgust I sprouted a whole new crop of freckles on my face. I even tried freckle cream in a fruitless attempt to make them less noticeable. At the boardwalk we hired a beach umbrella by the week in a futile attempt to keep the sun off our exposed skin.

I can't recall Mother ever going into the water. She sat on the beach knitting or sewing while she watched my brother and me play in the waves and sand. On the way home, at the end of the day we often walked out on the pier and bought fresh fish for our supper.

After we had been in Santa Cruz for six weeks, Father arrived for the last two weeks to take his vacation and help mother pack up for the trip home.

15

The Peddlers

Before the day of the automobile, which gave those who could drive a great deal of mobility, there was no dashing to the store every time a person needed something. Most people who lived in town did not own a horse and buggy unless it was needed for their business, such as a physician or a midwife.

Milk, fish, produce, bakery goods, ice, and various other specialized services came to our neighborhoods by way of delivery wagons on set schedules.

Our family was very modern because we owned an ice box. The iceman stopped whenever we placed the "ICE" card in the front window. He wore striped coveralls, a leather apron, leg guards and a piece of leather to cover his right shoulder. He dug his tongs into the ice, hoisted the block onto his shoulder, carried it into the kitchen, then placed the ice in the appropriate compartment of the ice box.

On hot days he gave a big chip of ice to children to suck on. In warm weather the ice wagon attracted kids the way honey attracts flies.

The ice house was located on the edge of town. During the dead of winter the workers traveled into the high mountains to small lakes that had frozen over. They spent a good part of the winter sawing out huge blocks of ice from the lakes, loading them on horse drawn sledges and hauling them out of the snow country. Once they were below the snow line, the ice was transferred onto wagons for delivery to the ice house in Oroville.

The building had thick double walls and doors, and sawdust insulation was packed between the inner and outer walls. Under the building there was a deep pit in the ground lined with concrete. In this compartment the slabs of ice were neatly stacked, layer upon layer. Between each layer three or four inches of sawdust was spread as additional insulation. It also prevented the ice from sticking together.

Families who weren't fortunate enough to have ice boxes had coolers. The cooler consisted of a set of shelves covered with screen. Burlap was draped over the screen. A copper pipe with small holes drilled in it was attached to a garden hose and placed around the top of the cooler to constantly drip water on the burlap.

The cooler hung in the shade of a tree in the backyard. It wasn't very efficient with one hundred-plus-degree weather all summer. With only a cooler a homemaker's leftover food didn't keep very long. But at least the cooler did keep the butter from melting into a yellow puddle.

We relied a great deal on peddlers for many of our needs. The vegetable man came twice each week and stopped in the middle of a block. When he rang his large hand bell, the housewives who needed fresh fruit or vegetables dropped what they were doing, picked up their change purses along with a basket, and hurried out to his wagon to buy things not grown in their own back yard gardens. Mother only bought such items as asparagus, cauliflower, bananas, and coconuts. Not every family had a vegetable garden, so they depended on the vegetable man for common things like string beans, carrots, and lettuce.

On Fridays the fish man arrived early in the morning. He announced his coming by the honking of a horn. He had a big brass instrument attached to the side of his wagon. It looked like a bugle with a big black rubber bulb attached where the mouthpiece should be. After each blast on the horn he shouted at the top of his lungs, "Fresh Fish." Each woman hurried out with a pail or platter to select a suitable variety of seafood for her family's Friday dinner.

Guided by the size of her family, a woman purchased either a whole or half fish, or if they were small fish such as smelt or trout, a few or many. Depending on what was in season—salmon, halibut, trout, sea bass, carp, or sole—the housewife made her decision on what variety of fish she intended to feed her family for their Friday dinner. Depending on the time of year, the fishmonger stocked fresh shellfish such as crabs, shrimp, oysters, and clams. The fish were displayed attractively on beds of crushed ice.

Once the selection had been made the fishmonger weighed it, and, if necessary, scraped off the scales, gutted it, then cut off the head and tail and filleted it or cut the fish into slices depending on the desire of the customer. The heads, tails, and bones were tossed into a barrel he carried for that purpose. He also kept a supply of water to wash the cleaned fish. He rinsed his hands before moving down the street to his next stop.

If his customers wanted to make a fish chowder, he gave away for free a couple of fish heads and two or three tails with a generous inch or two of meat attached. They were perfect for that purpose. Anyone who had a cat or two around the house received a package of scraps for the family pets.

The bakery wagon came by a couple of times a week. My family were not good customers as we did nearly all of our own baking. Now and then we children, if we happened to have an extra nickel burning a hole in our pocket, bought a cream puff, a maple bar, or a chocolate eclair. I admired the shelves loaded with mouth-watering cakes, pies, and cookies displayed in the back of the bakery wagon. Occasionally Mother bought one or two dozen cookies for unexpected company. I loved to be with her while she picked them out because a "Baker's Dozen" meant thirteen. Of course we children assumed the extra one was for us. The baker saved the broken cookies to hand out to those who stood around with a wistful look in their eyes.

The butcher's wagon came down our street every morning. We hoped he'd arrive before we left for school. We found that if we stood beside our mother and looked longingly enough as she bought her day's supply of meat, my brother and I usually ended up with a thick slice of bologna or a frankfurter to eat on our way to school.

Almost any home had a number of chairs with woven cane bottoms. There was a Chinese man in Oroville who came a couple of times a year to our neighborhood to reweave and repair cane-bottomed chairs. He carried his tools and all other items necessary for his work in two baskets suspended on each end of a pole. I loved to watch him work. His fingers seemed to fly as he crafted cane into intricate designs. His tools were his fingers and a sharp knife with which he wove the wet cane into a new chair seat. They were very durable and with proper care lasted the owner for years.

When the gypsies arrived in Oroville, they camped on the bank of the Feather River just outside the city limits. They looked for a flat, grassy spot where they could park their wagons and pushcarts and graze their stock. They sharpened knives and scissors, soldered or riveted handles back onto pots, and repaired leaking buckets and dish pans.

The gypsy tinkers were welcome when they came to Oroville, as most households had something put aside that needed mending or sharpening. Because of their dark complexion and nomadic life style, they were looked on with a certain amount of suspicion. No doubt about it, they were certainly different from the average citizen in our community. The men wore big, gold earrings and lively-colored neck scarves. They also had jet black beards and hair. The women wore brightly patterned skirts, loose blouses and, like the men, big gold earrings. I think the really difficult thing to understand about them was the fact they didn't have a regular home to live in and wandered from place to place. Their roots were in their clan so they were not dependent in any way on a particular locale.

We children were, at the same time, fascinated and scared by them. We were warned never to go near their camps as they were suspected of stealing children and turning them into gypsies, or even worse, of selling them. Of course they didn't really do this, but it made a good story and brought a measure of excitement and exotic intrigue to Oroville whenever they arrived in town.

All of the purveyors I've mentioned thus far conducted their business in town but couldn't hold a candle to the hawkers who made their rounds out on the farms. These peddlers had real class! They, and their colorful rigs pulled by powerful horses were elegant by any measure. The best of all of them was the dry goods peddler who brought fabric to Grandma Phoebe's farm.

Whoever saw him first called out "The Dry Good Peddler's coming!" That was all it took for Grandma Phoebe to take off her kitchen apron and put on a lace-trimmed, white apron. Then she stepped over to the kitchen mirror which had a comb tied by a string hanging from it. She quickly ran the comb through her hair. Once she had completed grooming herself, then, and only then, would she allow us to run out into the barnyard to make the peddler feel welcome.

The dry goods peddler who called on Grandma for many years was a small Jewish man who drove an enormous covered rig reminiscent of a circus wagon. Its covering was made of wood. It was enclosed front and back and had folding stairs in the rear. The entire rig was painted attractively in bright colors, including the spokes of the wheels. On the sides were generous scroll letters in gold leaf which announced, *DRY GOODS*. His outfit was drawn by a matched pair of elegant, powerful, Clydesdale draft horses.

He was short of stature—about five-feet tall—and very stylish in attire. He dressed in a black suit with a frock coat, gray spats over his black shoes, and a brightly colored vest of brocade complete with a heavy gold chain to which a fancy gold hunter's case watch was attached. This ensemble was topped off with a derby hat. He sported soft leather gloves while driving or hitching up his team. When he was on the road or working with his horses, he wore a long white duster to keep his outfit from becoming soiled. The pliable leather gloves were intended to keep his hands soft and clean. In that way he never soiled his merchandise while displaying it.

His normal routine was to call on two farms each day. If he came in the morning, he expected to be invited to stay for the noon meal. If he arrived in the afternoon, he stayed for supper and took for granted there was a place in the barn to feed and bed down his horses and for him to sleep.

When he came to Grandma's farm in the afternoon, she made sure there was a bucket full of hot water delivered out to the barn that evening and again in the morning so he could wash and shave. Grandma prided herself in seeing that he left her farm after eating a hearty breakfast. She made very sure the menfolk provided an ample supply of hay and oats for his horses.

This delightful little man so appreciated Grandma's kind and thoughtful treatment that he always presented her with a sort of ritual present as he was about to take his leave. This was usually a can of scented talcum powder or a bottle of cologne.

What merchandise he carried around in that wonderful and colorful wagon! He stocked everything and anything in the way of material or sundries a woman ever longed for from pins, needles, thread, and fancy buttons to silks, velvets, and the latest dress patterns from New York and Europe. He stored his wares in his wagon in black enameled tin cases with hinged tops trimmed in goldleaf scroll work.

These cases were brought into the house and arranged on the parlor floor. There were boxes of laces, ribbons, bolts of table damask, ginghams, taffetas, and a soft light cotton fabric called nainsook for fine women's undergarments and embroideries. Grandma had a heyday planning her next sewing projects as she made her selections.

Once Grandma was satisfied that she had made all of her choices, the peddler, with a great flourish, pulled out his order book to tot up the charges. When they had agreed on the total price, she ushered everyone out of her parlor. For some unexplained reason she allowed me to stay. After carefully shutting and locking the door, she opened the clock which doubled as the family bank. From her store of money she counted out enough gold and silver pieces to pay for her purchases. There was little if any paper money in Oroville in those days. With the exception of pennies and nickels made of copper and nickel, money was either silver or gold.

Grandma made very sure the peddler didn't see where the money came from. Of course any thief was well aware of the favorite places where farm wives hid their supply of ready cash.

After the dry goods peddler departed, the purchases were not put away for two or three days. They were arranged in an attractive way in the parlor so they could be handled and admired by everyone in the household.

Another hawker who came to the farm was the Watkins Man whose specialty was coffee and tea. He carried a full line of other Watkins products. These included extracts, such as vanilla, lemon, and peppermint. He stocked a variety of spices. He had items that were guaranteed to cure nearly everything. When asked, he came up with brews to alleviate any malady or affliction known to man or beast.

The Watkins Man was certainly a welcome visitor to the farm, but for excitement, showmanship, and style he couldn't hold a candle to the dapper, dry goods peddlers.

16

Liquor

In our town we had a number of citizens who were town drunks, or at least they were men who enjoyed overindulging in drink. These town characters were not the miners I mentioned earlier, who spent Saturday night in town getting drunk, raising hell, womanizing, and whooping it up. After their fling they staggered back to the miner's annex of the hotel, fell into bed and spent Sunday sleeping it off, not to be heard from again until the next weekend.

One town eccentric was a man who possessed grand good manners and courtesy. Colonel Parks, a veteran of the War Between the States where he had acquired his military title of Colonel, was one of our benign and genial town characters. From one day to the next, he was never completely drunk and never completely sober.

The Colonel had two daughters, both spinsters. One was a school teacher and the other was a music teacher who gave piano lessons. His wife worked as a practical nurse. The three women labored hard to keep the Colonel in the manner to which he had become accustomed.

During the late spring and throughout the summer months, the Colonel wore a white three piece linen suit, white buck shoes, and a cravat complete with a diamond stick pin. He topped things off with a white Panama hat. He completed his ensemble with a fresh cut flower in his lapel's buttonhole. He carried a polished mahogany walking stick with a sterling silver top which matched the case and stopper of his whiskey flask.

Each day he strolled grandly to the Courthouse Square where he spent time with his Grand Army of the Republic cronies discussing the news of the day, including the weighty and important affairs of the community, state and nation.

Then there was old Mr. Gaddy. His real name was Gadducci. He and his wife ran an Italian restaurant. His sons raised row crops and drove the vegetable wagon which supplied much of the town with fresh produce. Normally, and that was a good part of the time, he was sober. During his temperate periods he was a model husband and a happy, cheerful, and hard-working restaurateur.

Mr. Gaddy only became inebriated periodically. When he tied one on, he invariably was mean and bad-tempered and went out of his way to pick fights with anyone regardless of their size or age. When he went on a tear, the town constable was eventually called. Mr. Gaddy was strong as a bull when he was intoxicated. The constable usually had to draft a number of spectators to help subdue him. The upshot was that he regularly became an unwilling county guest and was locked up in the jail until he sobered up.

Occasionally, and only after he had been drinking, he was known to beat his poor wife unmercifully. There were no organizations such as Battered Women's Centers or Alcoholics Anonymous to help poor Mrs. Gaddy. Women were considered pretty much the property or chattel of their husbands. Anything short of killing his wife was accepted by the community as a regrettable but normal part of the relationship between a married couple.

Mrs. Gaddy suffered this cruel treatment silently as long as she could. Then one night she took matters into her own hands. In a single act of desperation she cured her husband of his destructive drinking habit.

Mr. Gaddy consumed too much vino and beat his wife. Afterwards, as usual, he fell into bed to sleep it off. Mrs. Gaddy waited patiently until her husband was sound asleep. She then slipped noiselessly out of bed and crept silently down the stairs to the wood box in the kitchen. Here she carefully selected a hefty stick of oak stove wood. Club in hand, she slipped back up the stairs and into the bedroom. With the piece of stove wood she beat Mr. Gaddy severely about his head and shoulders.

After her husband regained his senses she told him, "Mr. Gaddy, you are a very big man. I am a very small lady. I cannot stop you from beating me every time you get drunk." She then looked him square in the eyes and shook her improvised club at him. "Sometime, Mr. Gaddy, you have to sleep. When you do, I shall hit you as hard as I can!" She shook the stick at him again, "If your head gets broken and you die, I will be very sorry, but I want you to know, that I will hit you every time you get drunk and beat me!"

Mrs. Gaddy evidently convinced her husband that she was dead serious because that was the end of Mr. Gaddy's periodic drunks. He needed no psychological program to get the idea that his wife really meant business.

As far as I know my father became intoxicated only once in his entire life. This happened when he was in his early thirties and suffered a great deal from what was diagnosed as neuralgia, a nerve disorder which caused him acute pain.

In desperation to find a treatment that really worked, Father's physician and dentist put their heads together and decided the only cure for his ailment was to pull all of his teeth. This decision was made irrespective of the fact that Dad's teeth were in perfect condition.

Before the ordeal, the dentist gave him two big swigs of whiskey, and then proceeded to yank out his teeth.

After the operation, Dad, in excruciating pain, reeled into the grocery store where he had worked as a young man. His former boss took one look at him and decided there was only one way to kill the pain. So he proceeded to pour Dad a water tumbler full of whiskey. After he was sure that my father had consumed the entire dose, he bundled him into the back of a delivery wagon and drove him home. Mother took one look at him and let out a scream. After she had regained her composure she immediately put him to bed. It wasn't long before the pain, the shock from having his teeth pulled, and the whiskey combined and Father passed out. Father couldn't work for two weeks while he waited for the dentist to finish making him a set of teeth.

After that Father's painful affliction was cured. Not only was his neuralgia taken care of, but one unexpected outcome of this horrible experience was that it left him with a life-long dislike for the taste of whiskey.

From that day on he took an ounce of brandy in the morning rather than whiskey. In fact, after that, Mother substituted brandy in any recipe that called for whiskey. Even the taste of whiskey in a mince pie was distasteful to him.

At home, we had a fairly well-stocked liquor cupboard. For example, we served port wine in small glasses with cake or cookies when the Episcopal priest came calling. Claret was used in punch on very special occasions. A bottle of brandy was a part of the kitchen supplies, often as a flavoring in pudding sauces, fruit cake, and mince pies. Sherry was also used as a condiment and added to cream sauces for crab, shrimp, or chicken ala king. In the medicine cabinet stood a bottle of whiskey or brandy for eggnog, toothache, menstrual cramps or stomachache.

When a member of the family had one of these ailments, except for a toothache, a shot of liquor was served in a cup of hot water with some brown sugar and a dash of nutmeg. If you happened to be unfortunate enough to have a toothache, straight whiskey was held in the mouth until the pain went away. In the case of my brother and myself, once the pain had subsided we spit the whiskey into the toilet.

The only time whiskey was served in our home, other than for medicinal purposes, was on Christmas Eve, when the punch bowl was filled with eggnog and laced with a generous amount of whiskey or with brandy. On that occasion even we children were allowed to have some.

After Christmas we made a festive occasion of Epiphany which we called Twelfth Night. We regularly had a wassail bowl filled to the brim with hot mulled wine diluted with sweet apple cider. Friends and family gathered together to cut up the Christmas tree. We then burned it in our fireplace along with the wreath from the front door. At our home this was an annual party.

I can't think of any one of our friends and relatives who served liquor before meals. On special occasions we served port or sherry after a meal with dessert. To my knowledge, only the Italians in our community served wine with their meals.

In Oroville the Women's Christian Temperance Union, or the W.C.T.U. as they were known, was very active. The teetotallers signed their non-drinking pledge once a year. After that they smugly and self-righteously wore a little white ribbon pinned on their breasts for all the world to see.

17

Senior Citizens

T he term Senior Citizen was a term I had never heard until I became one myself. In my youth, old people were members of and usually a very productive and important part of virtually every family.

There were no retirement villages or nursing homes. Of course, Social Security and other schemes with all of their benefits, such as pensions, Medicare, disability insurance, unemployment insurance, workman's compensation, and so forth were unheard of until the New Deal of Franklin Roosevelt during the Great Depression of the 1930s.

The only benefits were those for veterans of the War of the Rebellion, which had come to be known as the Civil War, and much later the Spanish-American War. They had to be applied for by the veteran or his widow and were given out only after a great deal of investigation, red tape and paperwork. Grandma Westwood received a

Civil War widow's pension in the grand amount of fifteen dollars a month which was paid to her quarterly. When that forty-five dollar check came in, Grandma usually went on a buying splurge and bought gifts for members of the family. I have a hunch her pension paid for her endless supply of lemon drops, peppermints, and horehound lozenges which were available in a never-ending supply from her wonderful petticoat pocket.

When my mother's mother was widowed for the third time, I was only five years old. Her coming to live with us was not an unusual occurrence. Most of my friends had older relatives or old maid aunts living under their roof. In the case of Grandmother McDonald, she moved in with us because she needed the security of our family.

Families stuck together and loathed the idea of looking outside the family for help. Taking care of ones' own kin was a matter of pride. During the years she lived with us, Grandmother and Mother shared the housework, went together to card parties, lodge meetings, and afternoon teas. No baby-sitters were needed when Mother and Dad stepped out for the evening or went on a trip because Grandmother was there to take care of us. She was a needed, important, permanent part of our family.

Occasionally Grandmother went on visits to her other three daughters. She rarely stayed away more than two or three weeks. She was sorely missed by the entire family when she was away.

My Grandmother and Grandfather Westwood moved in with their son, my Uncle John, after his wife died, and they were needed to help raise his children. They lived on Uncle John's farm for the rest of their lives.

Moving out to the farm was a great sacrifice for them. Grandfather sold his blacksmith shop and their home; they left their friends and began a whole new way of life. But they were devoted to their son and his four teen-aged daughters. After all, what was more important to their peace of mind, preserving their life style or moving to the farm where they were needed? In turn, they were loved and cared for when they old and were no longer able to take care of themselves.

The situation for Great-uncle Sam and Great-aunt Sarah was very different. This family truly epitomized the idea of the extended family when their two younger daughters were married. Shortly after their weddings the girls and their new husbands moved into the family home. The entire upstairs of Uncle Sam's large Victorian home was remodeled into two apartments and turned over to the newlyweds. One of the bedrooms was transformed into a sitting room; later it was converted to a playroom for their children.

After Uncle Sam died, the combined families spent much of their time downstairs. When Aunt Sarah grew old and infirm, both families revolved around her, grandchildren, sons-in-law, and daughters. They anticipated her every want.

Another example of how the elderly were taken care of was that of a neighborhood widow lady who was failing badly from terminal cancer and needed help. The care of this unfortunate woman became a neighborhood responsibility. Friends and neighbors willingly took turns caring for her. Mother or Grandmother's turn came around once each month.

Whomever's turn it happened to be on any particular day went to her home about eight o'clock in the morning prepared to spend the next twenty-four hours serving her every wish. This included doing her housework, changing the bed, cooking her meals, doing the laundry and ironing, reading to her, and writing her letters. At the end of the day she was helped into bed and prepared for the night.

The care-giver spent the night watching over her until relieved at eight o'clock the next morning. All of the volunteers were either members of her church or lodge, close neighbors, or old friends.

What we now call rest homes were unheard of. We also didn't have an orphanage in Oroville. Each family took care of its own. They did this, willing or not. The important thing is that they did what had to be done.

There were a couple of boarding houses in town where four or five old folks without families were cared for. A few of the wealthier old folks lived down on Meyers Street at the Union Hotel. These unfortunate people were usually childless.

The old men of Oroville, with canes in hand, walked to the Courthouse Square each day except when it rained. They sat on the benches arguing, gossiping, and telling war stories. Others played checkers, discussed politics and religion, and second-guessed the politicians. Most of the men were retired businessmen or farmers now living in town, who were deeply interested in civic affairs. Their favorite activity, provided they hadn't gone deaf, was to attend any and all trials, civil or criminal, going on at the Courthouse.

One had to have paid his dues, so to speak, to secure a permanent spot on one of the benches. To be a part of the old men's group was much like belonging to a club. There were no rules, no membership cards, and no dues, but those men knew who belonged and who didn't. To fit in, he had to be either a war veteran or be a recognized old-timer in the community. If he could qualify on both counts, then so much the better.

One of their functions was to look out for one another. If a regular failed to show up at the appointed hour, those who did immediately made it their business to find out why their crony was missing.

Then there was the Poor Farm. Those who were sent there were pitiful folks without money and near the end of their lives. They didn't have families to see to their needs and wants. Most were miners who had tuberculosis, were crippled with arthritis, burned out from drink, or all of the above. An older physician took care of them and made regular visits to the farm.

In addition to the doctor's visits, the Ladies Aid Societies from the various churches went out from time to time to cheer up the old men with hymns and cookies. At Christmas the old duffers received a bag of toiletries, chewing tobacco, and candy.

The Poor Farm was probably the best home many of the miners had since they were young men still living at home. No self-respecting family allowed a relative to become a ward of the county.

18

Death

Death was a time when families came together to grieve and to deal with their loss while friends and neighbors took over the day to day needs of the bereaved.

Immediately after a death the news spread quickly through church groups, lodges, and neighborhoods. Things began to happen like magic. I never figured out exactly how the organization of this mission of compassion and mercy took place or who actually took charge of the exercise. The important thing is that people stepped in to help the bereaved family. No family which had sustained the loss of a loved one was expected to do any cooking or housekeeping from the moment the family member passed away until well after the funeral. Neighbors and friends brought in the meals and served them, washed the dishes, then cleaned up the kitchen and the dining room. Everyone pitched in to do whatever they could to be of help.

There were no funeral parlors. There were a couple of undertakers, but their services were entirely different from what we think of today. The names that come to mind are George Sovereign, A. A. Ward and Charles Topping. They served as county coroners and prepared bodies for burial as a sort of sideline. They also took care of the grave opening and would even order a marble headstone from Marysville or Sacramento.

If there was to be a delay before the funeral because family members had to come from a distance, the undertaker might be called upon to embalm the body. Most families didn't think of using the undertaker's services. The thought of having strangers handling the body of a loved one was not well accepted.

Women friends closed the deceased's eyes, then put a four-bit piece on each eye to keep it closed. After that they tied a bandage around the expired's mouth to keep the jaw shut until rigor mortis insured it would stay that way. Then they washed the body. If the deceased was a man and beardless, they shaved him. Otherwise they trimmed and combed out his beard and moustache. For a woman, they washed and set her hair.

After all the details had been taken care of, they dressed the corpse in his or her Sunday's best clothes. Once all of these preparations had been accomplished, the family was ushered into the bedroom to view the corpse which had been laid out on top of the bedspread.

On some occasions a photographer was called to photograph the deceased in repose. This was done especially when there was family who either lived too far away to come to the funeral or still resided in the old country. This was a fairly common practice during the

Civil War and continued on until after the turn of the century.

The men who had already measured the corpse went to the mercantile store or the undertaker's to pick out an appropriate burial box. Both places carried a supply of various sizes and qualities. Once the choice was made, the casket was delivered as soon as possible to the deceased's home. The men also brought back a supply of white candles and two sawhorses which were set up in the parlor to support the casket with the lid serving as the base. The women draped the saw horses with a few yards of black cotton crepe or panne velvet.

Then the men lifted the body into the box and arranged the corpse in a suitable attitude of repose. The coffin was carried down to the parlor and set on the makeshift bier, and candles were placed on small tables at the head and foot of the coffin. They burned throughout each of the nights the body was laid out.

After the preparations were completed, the body was ready for viewing. Streams of friends and neighbors entered the parlor to pay their last respects to the deceased.

The wake lasted through each of the long nights prior to the funeral. Friends and neighbors took turns sitting up with the body in the parlor. To keep watch is what the term *wake* means. The body and the members of the family were never left alone during the long and difficult nights before the funeral.

Once a mourner had spent a respectable amount of time in the parlor paying his or her respects in the presence of the corpse, he or she was expected to retire to the dining room or the kitchen to have a bite to eat.

Everyone was encouraged to partake from the generously donated food. Every surface in the dining room and kitchen fairly groaned with every imaginable assortment of casseroles, varieties of roasted joints, sliced meats, salads, cakes, and pies.

This was also a time to relate memories, usually pleasant or humorous, about the person now laid out in the parlor. If the deceased had suffered from a long and painful illness, it was usually agreed by all that he or she was much better off now and at rest.

A horse-drawn hearse conveyed the body to the church and eventually to the cemetery. If the deceased was a woman, paired white horses were furnished. For a man, two matched black horses pulled the hearse. When the funeral was for an infant or a small child, the tiny casket was normally carried to the cemetery by the parents in a four place surrey with the miniature casket tenderly placed across the knees of the grieving mother and father.

There were no floral shops in our town to prepare floral pieces for funerals. Neighbors made the flower arrangements, and Mother was a long time member of the floral committee. It was considered very important to have some sort of floral arrangements because flowers are the traditional symbol of a Christian's belief in the resurrection of the body.

Standard frames made of wood and chicken wire covered with dried moss were stored at the cemetery. These included a variety of shapes such as crosses, broken wheels, pillows, and stars. Once the appropriate selections were made, they were brought home and soaked in wash tubs. While this was going on, other women brought in laundry baskets full of fresh cut flowers and greenery. Ferns and ivy leaves went on first, then each flower was secured into the moss with small wires or hair pins. Finally a bow made of ribbon was attached at the appropriate place on each arrangement.

The flower committee turned out some beautiful floral pieces, especially when red, pink, and white oleanders were in bloom. In winter, when there were no fresh cut flowers available, the women used quantities of red ribbons and toyon berries arranged on beds of evergreens. In many ways the funeral pieces looked much like Christmas wreaths.

Before the funeral took place, the floral pieces were taken to the cemetery and placed around the freshly opened grave. Once the casket had been covered and the grave filled, they were lovingly placed over the mound of dirt and remained there until they had wilted.

On the appointed day, usually two to three days after death, depending on how far the next of kin had to travel to be there, the funeral took place. After the family had taken a last look at the corpse, men nailed or screwed the lid of the coffin shut. Then more friends loaded the casket into the hearse. If the church was close, the pallbearers might hoist the casket onto their shoulders and carry the body to the church for the service.

If the deceased was an important person in the community, the stores closed for the funeral and the town band turned out to lead the hearse to the cemetery. The Civil and Spanish-American War veterans wore their uniforms and served as guards of honor. If the deceased had belonged to the fire company, the firemen turned out in their uniforms. The same for anyone who belonged to a lodge. Townspeople walked behind the horse-drawn hearse to the graveyard. Everyone knew when the funeral was over because the band played lively tunes returning to town.

The Roman Catholics had their own cemetery with consecrated ground. The Jews also had a separate plot as did the Chinese. Everyone else was buried in the town cemetery.

The Chinese were buried in Sovereign's Cemetery south of Oroville. Here the Chinese were temporarily buried until a certain specified number of years had passed; then their bones were exhumed and prepared to be returned to their family home in China.

The Chinese funerals were not attended by anyone I knew, but we always made our way up to Broderick Street to watch the goings-on. The funeral procession headed away from the Chinese Temple in the direction of their own cemetery. A huge dragon with a number of men inside danced in front of the highly decorated funeral cortege. Behind the dragon dancers, men scattered colored squares of paper with little holes in them on the street. I was told that they believed the devil had to crawl through each and every hole before he could reach the soul of the deceased. It was hoped that by the time he reached the person's soul, it would be safely in heaven.

Many of the Chinese women weren't capable of walking behind the casket as their feet had been bound when they were babies and walking was painful and virtually impossible. They followed behind the procession in a surrey. The women dressed in white, which signified mourning.

Another Chinese custom was to leave food such as pork, rice, and sweets on the grave. This was done to give the deceased something to eat while being transported to heaven. It was a common practice for tramps at night to sneak out to the Chinese cemetery to eat the food.

It was the practice in most families with European backgrounds, to go into public mourning following the death of a loved one. The piano, except for the mandatory daily practice of the youngsters, was locked for the next twelve months. The same was true of the pump organ. Women wore black. Men wore a black band on their left sleeve for one solid year. Older women who had lost their husbands wore black for the remainder of their lives, although they usually added white collars and cuffs after the official year of mourning was completed.

In 1904 Grandma Westwood came out of her year of deep mourning. At that time she had some purple velvet pansies sewn onto her bonnet. She was sure Grandpa wouldn't mind a little extra color on her dress, as he liked to see her dressed up and knew how much she loved pretty things.

19

Epilogue

I was goaded into writing this account by my children and especially by two of my grandsons, George and Charles Rohrbacher. They were so keenly interested in life during the late 1800s and early 1900s and so pleased that I still remembered things so vividly that they bombarded me with questions every time they came to visit me.

I am very gratified that it was my good fortune to be born in the United States and to have been a citizen of this great nation. I am also thankful that I have enjoyed a relatively long life and have seen the fascinating changes that have taken place during my allotted time on this earth.

I left Oroville in 1914 to attend the University of California at Berkeley. The first day I was on the Berkeley campus I met the man who was later to become my husband. Brother Bill helped me, a lowly freshman, make it through the registration line at Wheeler Hall. While we were there, a fraternity brother of Bill's from Stockton, California, slipped into line with us. We were introduced and by the time we had made it to the registration desk, he had asked me for our first date.

I looked to my brother for a sign that this rather brash and forward, pre-medical student friend of his was okay before I consented to go out with him. He gave his nod of approval and there and then, in the registration line that September of 1914, began a close friendship. Little did I know that four years later he would become my one and only marriage partner. His name was George Henri Rohrbacher.

At the university I majored in biology, and despite the discouraging remarks from everyone I knew, including my professors, I fully intended to matriculate at the end of my junior year from the Berkeley campus to U.C.'s medical school in San Francisco. I suppose I was somewhat ahead of my time, but those were my intentions and I worked blamed hard to earn the necessary grades to complete my dream. I carried a straight 'A' average in all of my classes except one. I had the misfortune to take organic chemistry from a professor who prided himself at never having given an 'A' to any student during his entire tenure as a professor at the University of California. I settled, reluctantly, for a 'B+.'

But my dream of becoming a physician was not to be fulfilled. On April 6, 1917, the United States declared war on Germany. This was near the end of my junior year and Henri's first year in medical school and his senior year in college. In those days it only took three years of pre-med to matriculate to medical school. The senior year was done as a first year medical student and the B.S. Degree was awarded at the end of that year. Henri immediately withdrew from medical school and enlisted in the U.S. Navy as a medical corpsman. After boot camp he was assigned aboard the *U.S.S. Northern Pacific,* a troop transport taking troops to France. At this point in our relationship we were very much in love and contemplated marriage when the war was over.

Phoebe Louise Westwood (1896-1984) and George Henri Rohrbacher (1893-1955) on their wedding day, September 18, 1918. *(Rohrbacher Family Collection)*

Eventually Henri was sent to Officers' Candidate School at the Naval Academy at Annapolis, Maryland. During the summer of 1918 he was commissioned an ensign in the Navy. In September of that year we were married. Immediately after the war ended, with my encouragement, Henri left the Navy and returned to medical school. By that time I had completed work on my degree.

We made our home in San Francisco close to the U.C. Medical Center while I accepted a teaching position in the Oakland school system to earn enough money to put my newly demobilized husband through medical school. For the next five years we lived a no-frills life. After the first World War there was no such thing as a G.I. Bill to help returning servicemen get on with their education.

Each morning I took the ferry across the bay to Oakland to teach. During summer vacations we both worked like the devil to sock away enough money to take care of the bare essentials such as clothing and other things my paltry teacher's salary could not cover. I continued teaching during the next four years until Henri received his M.D. degree and then finished his internship. In June of 1924 he graduated from the University of California's Medical School. He took his Medical Boards and received one of the highest scores ever registered at that time. In May of that year we had the first of four children. From that time on, the main purpose and direction of my life was to help my husband set up his medical practice and become an established physician in his hometown of Stockton.

We bought a small, five-room house on North Regent Street in Tuxedo Park and over the years it expanded, as did our family, until it had a total of five bedrooms. There was some type of construction going on most of the time. Each time I thought of expanding our home, my husband jokingly referred to me as his "Mrs. Winchester."

We eked out a living through the Great Depression only to have World War II come along and disrupt our lives. Henri held the rank of Lt. Colonel as a medical officer in the California National Guard. When the 40th Division was called to active duty in 1941, he reluctantly closed the practice he had struggled so hard to establish and went off to war for a second time.

World War II took a heavy toll on my personal life. Not only did I send my husband off to the South Pacific, but eventually I sent my oldest son, George, to serve, and finally my youngest son, Richard, who was not quite fifteen when the war started.

My husband left the United States in March of 1942 aboard the *Queen Elizabeth I* and returned home in the spring of 1945.

Shortly after my husband shipped out, I took over the duties of the Chief Hostess of all of the Service Clubs and Guest Houses at Camp Cooke, California. Many of the armored divisions who later fought in North Africa, Italy, and Europe were trained at this army camp.

During my tenure with the Service Clubs I was responsible for the day-to-day operation of all of the club facilities and the Guest Houses. I also had the honor of meeting with and hosting numerous Hollywood celebrities, band leaders, and broadcast personalities who came to entertain the troops. Many of the major radio shows were broadcast from Camp Cooke.

I had a very responsible position which gave me a purpose while my husband was overseas. I held that assignment until the war started to wind down, and then it was time for me to reopen our home in Stockton.

When my husband returned from the Pacific, he was physically broken and a disillusioned man. He left me a widow at the early age of fifty-seven.

Now that I have lived nearly eighty-six years, I have to admit that my lifetime, to quote Charles Dickens, has spanned "the best of times and the worst of times." I must say that life while I was growing up was certainly different from what it is today. In many ways conditions were better then than now, and in many ways they were much worse. I'll be frank. I have little patience with those who speak of the "good old days," because, as you've read in my description of my formative years, the old days weren't that good, just different.

During my lifetime I have found that progress is pretty constant. Of course, a great deal of change has taken place during my life. Any list of the most significant changes which have occurred over these years is of necessity only partial.

I started in life during the tail end of the so-called Victorian era and all that it implies. Then, in rapid succession came the Spanish-American War, the telephone, electricity, airplanes, the assassination of President William McKinley, the federal income tax, World War I, the suffragette movement, the Prohibition Amendment, the Bolshevik Revolution, moving pictures, the age of the flapper, women's vote in the U.S., radio broadcasting, political scandals, speakeasies, gangsterism, the Great Depression, child labor laws, Coxey's Army, The New Deal, the rape of Nanking, World War II, penicillin and sulfa drugs, rationing, the cruelty of the Japanese toward

Allied prisoners of war, the horrors of the German death camps, Hiroshima and Nagasaki, the Atomic and Hydrogen Age, television, The Fair Deal, the Cold War, Joseph Stalin, Red China, The Iron Curtain, the Korean War, racial problems, integration of the South, polio vaccine, the assassination of President John F. Kennedy, space travel, The Great Society, The Vietnam War, the moon walk, heart transplants, street drugs, double-digit inflation, the resignation of a Vice-President and then a President, the AIDS epidemic, and much more.

Despite the terrible and devastating events that have happened during my lifetime I have some wonderful things to look back on.

I have had the pleasure of rearing four children and getting to know twelve grandchildren and five great-grandchildren. This is a legacy in and of itself and is nearly enough accomplishment for any one woman's life.

In conclusion, I'll do my best to give my philosophy of life in as few words as possible. Despite the many failures of humankind during my existence, I have observed some progress. I truly hold out tremendous hope for future generations. My only regret is that I won't be around to find out what they do with the world my generation has left to them.

Phoebe Louise Westwood Rohrbacher (1896-1984)